sustainable crafts,
gifts and
projects

FOR ALL SEASONS

sustainable crafts, gifts and projects

FOR ALL SEASONS

Becci Coombes

WHITE OWL

AN IMPRINT OF PEN & SWORD BOOKS LTD.
YORKSHIRE – PHILADELPHIA

First published in Great Britain in 2023 by
Pen & Sword WHITE OWL
An imprint of
Pen & Sword Books Ltd
Yorkshire – Philadelphia

ISBN 9781399064330

Printed and bound in China by 1010 Printing International Limited

Photography by Becci Coombes
Design: Paul Wilkinson

Pen & Sword Books Limited incorporates the imprints of Atlas, Archaeology, Aviation, Discovery, Family History, Fiction, History, Maritime, Military, Military Classics, Politics, Select, Transport, True Crime, Air World, Frontline Publishing, Leo Cooper, Remember When, Seaforth Publishing, The Praetorian Press, Wharncliffe Local History, Wharncliffe Transport, Wharncliffe True Crime and White Owl.

For a complete list of Pen & Sword titles please contact:
PEN & SWORD BOOKS LIMITED
47 Church Street, Barnsley, South Yorkshire, S70 2AS, England
E-mail: enquiries@pen-and-sword.co.uk
Website: www.pen-and-sword.co.uk

Or
PEN AND SWORD BOOKS
1950 Lawrence Rd, Havertown, PA 19083, USA
E-mail: Uspen-and-sword@casematepublishers.com
Website: www.penandswordbooks.com

CONTENTS

INTRODUCTION

There is a certain joyous rhythm to the passing of the seasons, and each one brings its own pleasures. From long, lazy picnics in the golden grasses of summer, to the crisp crunch of autumn and the burn of breath on a white frosty day, all have their own delights, and few things are more enjoyable than a wander through the ever-changing countryside, searching for interesting things to forage for food or take home for crafts.

This book is divided into four chapters covering the seasons, and each one features recipes, activities and craft projects with which to make the most of nature's gifts. One of the wonderful things about these projects is that to a certain extent you have to be in rhythm with the year. There is no making dandelion honey in January for example, so a degree of patience is necessary; watching the months turn and waiting for the next opportunity to slowly swing past is its own pleasure. I would also add it is important you know that I have no formal culinary training whatsoever; the recipes included here are those beloved by our family, so please tweak them as you see fit!

A SHORT NOTE ABOUT MATERIALS

I have tried to ensure that the majority of materials and ingredients used in this book can be found at home and repurposed, whether in your craft corner, kitchen cupboard or wardrobe; friends and family are always a great resource too, as most people are always keen to pass some of their unwanted textiles or household junk on to someone who would like it.

Where items do need to be purchased, they should be readily available from your local craft shop, charity shop or hardware store; some ingredients (such as glycerine) are used in more than one project so buying in bulk is not only more economical but reduces waste. Growers of willow and bamboo sell their rods and canes in foot lengths, so measurements are in imperial. If you buy a bundle though, it will be weighed in kg!

I have also tried to steer away from anything plastic; for example,

rather than using polystyrene wreath bases, advice is given on how to make alternatives out of recycled materials. (Any tips given in brackets mean slightly less successful moments are possible, and I have negotiated my way through them so you don't need to!)

Likewise, the majority of the tools used in this book should be found in most homes; the only exception is the metal-stamping equipment used for the windchimes, but not only is this entirely optional, if you do decide to purchase it you'll find it useful for no end of projects and gifts.

FORAGING

Many of the foraged ingredients for the ideas in this book should be available in your garden or local hedgerows. In terms of foraging and the law, in the UK it is illegal to dig up wild plants, fungi or lichen; there is also a fairly long list of species which are protected from intentional picking or removal. However, although permission should always be sought from a private landowner when picking wild foods, it is largely acceptable in public spaces such as beaches, woodland and parks. I have endeavoured to only include wildflowers and berries that are not only commonplace but abundant and easily recognised, such as blackberries, dandelions and rosehips.

There are a few rules to remember when foraging: only take as much as you need, and try to spread out your picking so you don't deplete just one area. Avoid areas of high traffic pollution and always harvest away from areas where dogs might have been active. Lastly, accurate identification is essential, especially when it comes to poisonous plants, fungi and berries; there are many apps and online resources available to help make sure you are picking the right thing, and a weekend foraging course is always a fun and educational experience. In the US the laws can vary more widely from state to state, especially with regard to national parks, so do please check your local regulations.

Spring

CRYSTALLISED SPRING FLOWERS

Edible flowers add a pretty burst of colour to any bake. Spring flowers may only bloom for a couple of weeks before the season moves on, so this is a splendid way to preserve them for use on summer cakes, iced biscuits and celebration puddings. Once thoroughly dried out they should last for up to six months if stored in an airtight tin.

Many spring plants from your garden are suitable for crystallising; primroses are edible, as are violets, mint leaves, forget-me-not flowers and borage. Pick the flowers on a dry sunny morning and leave them somewhere safe for a few minutes to allow any little bugs to make their escape; don't use flowers from garden centres as they may well have been sprayed with chemicals.

Materials

- 1 egg white
- Caster sugar
- Kitchen paper
- A clean paintbrush

Method

1. Prepare your materials. Tip the egg white into a bowl, add one teaspoon of water and whisk with a fork until gently frothy.

2. Pour some caster sugar into a second bowl and line a tray with kitchen paper.

3. Remove the green stem from one of the flowers then paint it on both sides with egg white so that it is completely covered (but not

soggy), ensuring that you wiggle the brush into every nook and cranny. I find it easiest to hold primroses and violets on the palm of my hand with the stalk trapped between two fingers, whereas the tiny forget-me-nots are best painted straight on to kitchen paper.

7. Sprinkle caster sugar over the flower so every surface is covered, then lay it face down to dry for 24 hours. Repeat with the rest.

8. Store your sugar flowers in layers of kitchen paper in an airtight tin, hidden in a cool place for up to six months. Use to decorate cupcakes and desserts, or garnish cocktails; I had to make three batches of mint leaves for this project as every time I turned round they had been eaten by teenage boys.

SILVER BIRCH BIRD'S NEST

Weaving twigs into a small artwork is always a satisfying way to spend an hour in the garden on a bright warm spring morning, without doing anything as unpleasant as actual heavy digging. Silver birch is a great resource for wreath and nest-making as the twigs stay fairly flexible for ages and are easily collected from the ground after a windy night, but any bendy twigs will work well. The nest should last indefinitely, and looks beautiful as a rustic bowl later in the year, filled with autumnal fruit or pine cones, sprigs of greenery and a few vintage baubles. Or car keys and half a packet of chewing gum.

Materials

A good armful of silver birch twigs (these projects always take more material than you think!)

- A few other twigs with green shoots
- Moss (either dried reindeer moss or foraged from the garden)
- 6 eggs (the paler the better as they will show the colour more)
- Blue food colouring
- Vinegar
- Secateurs

NOTE: Once they have been dyed, the eggs can be used for cooking up to the end of their marked shelf life.

Method

1. Firstly, dye your eggs. Simply stir a good healthy dollop of blue food colouring into a litre of cold water before adding 2 tablespoons of vinegar. Immerse the eggs carefully with a spoon and then leave for up to an hour so they turn a beautiful shade of blue. I removed these at twenty-minute intervals so they were all slightly different shades.

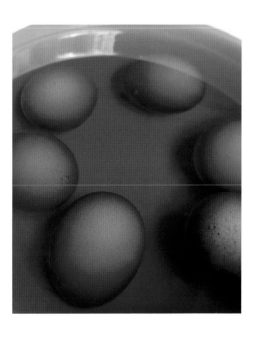

2. Give them a quick rinse and leave on a plate without touching them too much until they are dry (you might want to wear gloves for this as they will stain your fingers when wet).

3. Take a long flexible twig and bend it into a circle, then twine both the stem and the tip around the ring to make a mini wreath (here my initial twig frame measures roughly 30cm).

4. Add another twig, inserting it from front to back with the butt (bottom end) pointing to the left, then winding the long length around the ring towards the right. I always add new sticks to a wreath in the same direction as it gives a lovely even twist to the finished form. Don't worry about any stray twigs as everything can be trimmed at the end.

5. Continue to work your way around the circle, weaving in more material until you have a sturdy wreath; at this point you could pop in a few catkins or pussy willow sprigs and hang it on your front door, but if you would like to make a nest then we will need to add a base.

6. Holding both sides of the wreath, pull the sides up gently to give a little height.

7. Now taking a thinner twig, push it down through into the ring at 6 o'clock and back up at 12 o'clock, so essentially you are filling in the base of the nest like spokes on a wheel.

8. Continue working around the circle until the base is filled. I find it easiest to hold the side of the nest and wiggle my thumb and middle finger together to find a little space to thread the twigs through.

9. Once the base has been filled, line the nest with moss. Strip the lower leaves from your green twigs and insert them into the woven twigs, ensuring they are going in the same direction as the silver birch.

10. Trim any wild twiggy pieces you feel are uncontrollable, then add your eggs and tuck in any other little foraged sprigs you find pretty (I added a few little touches of early cow parsley to add a frothy softness to the table centre).

EGGSHELL CANDLES

Eggshell candles are a great way to use up soy wax you may have left over from other projects, and are also a fabulous opportunity to display all those attractive vintage egg cups that lurk unused at the back of the kitchen cupboard. I had the good fortune to find these beautiful naturally pastel-coloured eggs at a local farm shop; the downside of free-range eggs is that the shells can be much more fragile than the standard supermarket brown variety (as you can see in the photograph, I did lose a few unexpected pieces!). If you can't find coloured ones locally, brown eggs can easily be dyed using the method outlined in the bird's nest project.

Materials
- 6 eggs
- 30g soy wax chips per egg
- Empty egg box
- 8cm votive cotton wicks with tabs
- Hot glue gun
- Cocktail sticks

Method

1. Prepare the eggshells; I have found that the easiest way to crack the eggs neatly is to give them a sharp tap with a table knife towards the pointed end; if you remove the broken pieces you can then tip the white and yolk out easily without them breaking (perfect for a chocolate mousse – see below for recipe), before nibbling away gently at the rest of the shell to get an even shape.

2. Remove any membrane from inside the shells by soaking them in warm soapy water for half an hour or so; if you put your thumb inside and gently rub the membrane, working your way gradually around the shell, you will find it comes off nicely.

3. Allow the eggs to dry thoroughly and then heat your glue gun. Apply a generous blob of adhesive to the metal tab on the wick and press it on to the base of the shell, moving it into place with a pencil if necessary.

4. Place the shells into an empty egg carton and lay a cocktail stick across each one to help centre the wick.

5. Soy wax can be successfully melted in a ceramic bowl in the microwave, but I still use the old-fashioned double boiler method; I have a metal jug reserved just for this purpose as it makes it much easier to pour without any messy drips. Stand your bowl or jug full of wax in a pan of water and bring to a simmer, stirring occasionally until all the chips have dissolved. Allow to cool for a few minutes before carefully filling the eggshells three-quarters full.

6. Give the eggs a little gentle tap to release any air bubbles, and then straighten the wicks if necessary (they can go a bit floppy when the hot wax is poured in). Re-centre them using the cocktail sticks as props, then set aside overnight to cool and harden.

7. Trim the wicks to 0.5cm and they are ready to light.

8. If you fancy trying your hand at coloured candles, the wax can easily be dyed with food colouring. Gel, paste or powder all work well (the liquid variety won't work as it will not blend with the wax successfully); just add a few drops to the melted wax before pouring and continue as normal.

9. The table centrepiece pictured was the result of a few minutes of foraging in the garden and kitchen cupboard. I filled an assortment of little vintage glasses with moss to hold the eggs securely and then laid them on a waterproof tray. A few more pieces of garden moss were tucked around the bottom of the glasses and then some primroses, borage and forget-me-nots scattered over the greenery (I poked the stems down into the moss with a pencil). Lastly, a few silver birch twigs were added to give a little drama and some water poured into the bottom of the tray to keep the display nice and damp.

Chocolate Mousse Recipe

Melt 25g of butter and 100g of dark chocolate in a microwave or bain-marie. Allow to cool slightly then stir in 3 egg yolks and set aside. Whisk the 3 egg whites until they form soft glossy peaks, sprinkle over 2 tablespoons of caster sugar and whisk again. Gently fold one quarter of the whisked whites through the chocolate mixture, then add the rest gradually, taking care not to knock the air out. Spoon into four little glasses and chill for at least 6 hours before serving with a scattering of raspberries. If you want to use all 6 eggs, remember to double these quantities!

FORAGED TWIG PLATTER

I love working with willow, and usually make these platters from soaked brown rods; however, as I was wandering around the garden in late April looking for primroses, I spotted many promising shoots sprouting up from all the hedges and thought a foraged platter might be fun. The tray will last all year, and is an unusual and attractive way to serve everything from freshly sliced bread to hard cheese and chutney (you could even make tiny ones; packaged as a rustic soap dish with a bar of handmade soap they would make a lovely gift).

Materials

- Secateurs
- A selection of long supple shoots
- Two lengths of ivy, jasmine or honeysuckle (failing that, jute twine makes a splendid alternative)

Method

1. Collect a selection of shoots and hedge trimmings from the garden (I cut 1-metre lengths from dogwood, plum, apple, willow and ash, plus a few pieces of blackcurrant).

2. Prepare your materials by roughly stripping away any leaves from the rods.

3. Take a long supple length of willow and shape it into a circle, tucking the ends in so it forms a wreath shape.

4. Rotate the wreath 180 degrees and feed another rod in from front to back so the butt (bottom end) is poking in the same direction as the first one. Weave the willow in and out of the ring to make the form sturdy, then snip off the ends.

5. The ring should be quite springy so push the sides in until you are happy the shape is circular.

6. Take four more lengths and lay them across the ring in two pairs.

7. Now we start to weave! Take a rod and, starting at right angles to the pairs, pass it over the wreath, under the first pair, over the second and lastly under the ring again.

8. Insert another length, this time working it first under the wreath and then over. Each rod you insert will go in the opposite order to the one next to it, thus giving you a lovely tactile basket structure. As more and more lengths are woven in, the tension of the rods starts to hold the platter together.

9. You may find it is more difficult to pass the twigs up and down through the structure as the work progresses, so save a few smaller ones for the sides.

10. Snip off all the untidy ends, making sure you leave the longer end pairs.

8

8

9

10

11. To finish the platter with rustic handles, cross the end pairs over each other. Take a piece of jasmine or other vine and hold the first 2cm against the crossed twigs. Wrap the long end around the crossed twigs a few times so that it holds them together and covers the short end, before tucking it underneath the wraps and pulling it through. Pull tight and snip off any excess.

12. Alternatively, you can cut off the end pairs neatly underneath the wreath to give you a circular plate – perfect for serving fruit or bread at a family meal, or as a foraging basket. As the twigs dry out over time they will shrink a little, so if you find they come loose you can either poke in a few more, or the easier (and lazier option) is to just fix them in place with a couple of blobs of hot glue from underneath.

DANDELION HONEY

Dandelions (Taraxacum officinale) are a wonderful sight in late spring and early summer, as their sunny little faces proliferate across garden and hedgerow. Traditionally used as a herbal treatment for digestive issues, liver health and as a diuretic, they are packed full of antioxidant, antiviral and antibacterial properties, and, best of all, can be foraged for free. Young tender leaves can be added to salads (although they do grow bitter as they get tougher), the roots dried to make a coffee substitute and the flowers fermented into country wines. Dandelion honey is my favourite way to use the blooms, with the fragrant confection having a taste and texture similar to honey. Spoon over scones and cream, pour over pancakes, spread over croissants and toast, or use as a filling in a Victoria sandwich; I particularly love it with Greek yoghurt and muesli.

As with all foraging, ensure the plants have not been sprayed with any chemicals and are picked from a dog-free area. The flowers are also beloved of bees as unusually they contain both nectar and pollen so try not to pick too many from any one spot. The one main issue with harvesting them is that as they grow very close to the ground, picking them involves a lot of bending down; for this reason, I would suggest involving the help of some younger family members who can just crawl efficiently across the grass. If you don't

get enough petals on your first foray, you can always pop them in the freezer until you have gathered enough for the recipe.

Ingredients (makes 4 or 5 jars)
- 150 dandelion heads
- 500g jam sugar (or granulated with 85ml liquid pectin)
- 500ml water
- 1 tablespoon lemon juice
- Sterilised jam jars

Method

1. Leave the flowers spread out on a garden table for a few minutes so any little creatures can make their escape. Don't wash them, as this will remove the pollen.

2. Preparing the dandelions is probably the fiddliest part of this recipe so again I would utilise the labour of helpful children. Remove the petals either by snipping them off with scissors or by tearing the flowerheads in half and then pulling the petals out; the object is to remove them without including any of the green bracts, as this can make the jam bitter.

3. Place the petals (bar a scant handful) in a large pan, add the water and bring to the boil. Simmer for a couple of minutes then allow to cool and steep overnight to make a dandelion tea.

4. If you don't have a sugar thermometer, now is the time to pop a saucer in the fridge. Pour the dandelion tea through a fine mesh sieve, squeezing the petal pulp with a spoon to extract as much liquid as possible, before discarding the petals. Measure the strained tea and if necessary top it back up to 500ml with water.

5. Add the tea, lemon juice and sugar to a large pan and place on the hob, stirring until all the sugar has been dissolved.

6. Now add the remaining petals, bring the mixture to a rolling boil (stir in the liquid pectin if using) and continue to boil until the jam has either reached 104–105°C or it passes the wrinkle test. To do this, drip a little of the jam on to the cold saucer and leave it to cool; it should wrinkle when pushed gently with your finger.

7. Leave the honey to cool for 15 minutes before skimming any scum off the top and potting into warm sterilised jars and labelling.

TOOTHBRUSH RAG RUG

As spring beckons, one's heart often tends towards a little cleaning and the hitherto unnecessary re-organisation of cupboards; should you find a quantity of bed linens you no longer fancy, they can easily be upcycled into gorgeous textiles. The joy of these tactile rugs is that no special materials are required, and you can set to work as soon as you fancy. Rather than being knotted on to a hessian backing or stitched together using a sewing machine, rags are threaded on to a chunky needle and essentially joined together using a simple half hitch; you don't even need to buy a special rug tool but can make one easily from bits and pieces around the home.

Traditionally made by Amish craftspeople, toothbrush rugs were so called as they were made using a needle created from a wooden toothbrush, which often had a hole at one end for hanging. The brush end would be sawn off and shaped to a point while the hanging hole made the eye. However, as I didn't really want to go and buy a wooden brush just for the purpose of sawing it in half, I began to explore other options, some more successful than others!

Initially, I began this rug with a needle which was 3D printed from corn starch, but when this snapped, an emergency substitute made from the wire cage on a champagne bottle and some duct tape turned out to be far superior. If your length of wire is stiff enough, you can bend the needle into a gentle 'C' shape which makes it easier to scoop between the knots. However, my favourite needle by far is one created from a solitary chopstick rattling around in the bottom of the kitchen drawer; three or four tiny holes were drilled next to each other in the wider end to create an oval eye, perfect for threading wide strips of fabric.

A longer-term project than many of the others in this book, it is perfect for whiling away the evenings, and as your work gets bigger it will helpfully keep your knees warm on those chilly spring evenings. Happily, the rugs are as machine washable as the fabric you use to make them so are ideal for pretty bathroom mats (although I would put them on a gentle wash); smaller mats can be popped inside a pillowcase to give them a little protection. Dry them flat, easing them back into shape by stretching and pulling gently as you go.

Materials

A selection of cotton or polyester fabrics such as duvet covers, sheets etc.
- Ruler
- Fabric scissors
- Felt tip pen
- Clipboard/safety pin and lap tray
- Needle of your choice

Method

1. Prepare your needle. If using a chopstick, drill a hole in the chunky end (I used a 2mm drill bit and then just kept making more holes next to each other until I was happy with the shape). To make a wire needle, cut a length of stiff 1mm wire to about 15cm long, and fold the ends to the middle. Secure the ends by wrapping with duct tape or sticky tape, then twist one end to make the point of the needle; leave the other end open to act as the eye.

2. Now let's turn our attention to the fabric; this project is very fabric hungry so it is well worth asking friends and family if they have any unloved bedding you could add to your stash. An average double duvet cover should result in a circular mat measuring roughly 65cm. Tear the

duvet cover into two separate halves, and then rip off any seams so you have two large rectangles of fabric.

3. Taking the first piece of material, mark along one edge every 4cm with the felt pen before cutting a small 1cm snip at every mark (the wider the strips the sturdier the rug and the more fabric required). If you would prefer to work with shorter pieces, cut the snips along the longer edge. However, I tend to make them along the shorter edge; this gives longer strips so that I won't have to join new pieces in so often and thus hide quite so many knots at the back of the work.

4. Carefully rip the fabric into 4cm strips, rolling them into little bundles and removing any loose threads as you go. Repeat with the second piece of duvet cover (I would heartily encourage family members to help with this part of the process so you can crack on with the fun part of actually making the rug).

5. To start the rug, take your first strip and fold it in half. Attach the fold to your clipboard, or if you don't have one, fix it to your trousers or a cushion using a safety pin.

6. The rug is made from a series of half hitches using a working cord (which as its name suggests does all the zipping about) and a filler cord, which just sits there happily and provides a base to work on.

7. Attach the needle to the left-hand strip to make the working cord. Take it out to the left in a loop and cross it over the filler, to make a number four.

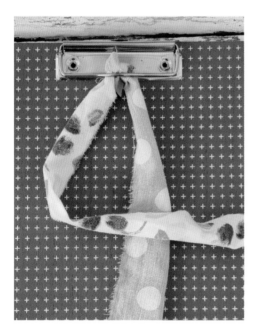
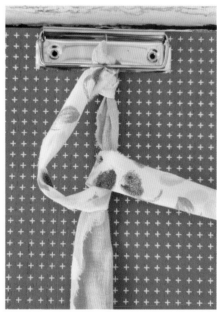

8. Now pass the needle underneath the filler cord and up through the loop, pulling it tight to form your first half hitch (also a blanket-stitch for those of you who love embroidery!).

9. Tie five more knots and then remove the work from the clipboard/safety pin.

10. Bend the work round into a circle. Take the filler up to the right and tuck it out of the way, then push your needle down

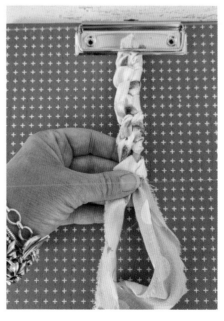

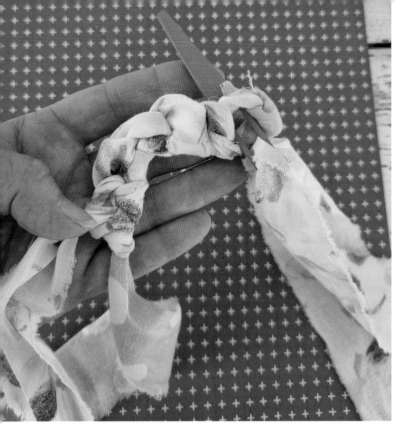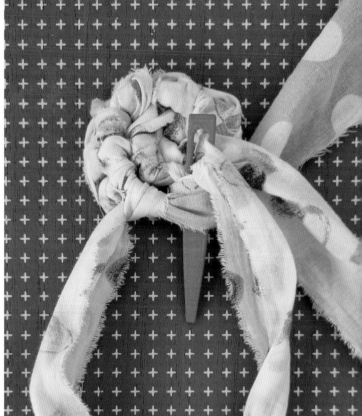

through the very first hole you made and pull tight to make a ring. Turn the circle over.

11. Continue to knot the rug by keeping the filler held tight against the circle, off to the right (you might find it useful to keep it bundled up so it doesn't get in the way too much). Push the needle down through the next hole then back up through the loop you have just made, before pulling it tight. This is where the clipboard or lap tray comes in useful, as the hard surface gives you something to push against whilst tightening the knot, helping to keep it even.

12. As the rug gets larger, you will need to add in extra stitches so that the work will lie flat and not take on a bowl shape. There is no hard and fast rule as to when to add them, but you will be able to tell when you need one initially as the hole by your next working stitch will seem larger. Pop an extra stitch in this gap and then continue as before; if the edge of the mat is curving up you will need to add a few more here and there, whereas if it has a wavy edge don't add any more for a while; after a couple of rounds you should be able to judge it! More stitches will need to be added in this way when the rug is still very small, as the curve is tighter, but as it progresses far fewer will be required.

13. Sooner or later your fabric strips will start to run out, but attaching a new one is very simple. Take a new strip and fold 2cm over at the end. Snip a 1cm cut into the fold and open it back out again. Repeat this process with the strip that is about to run out.

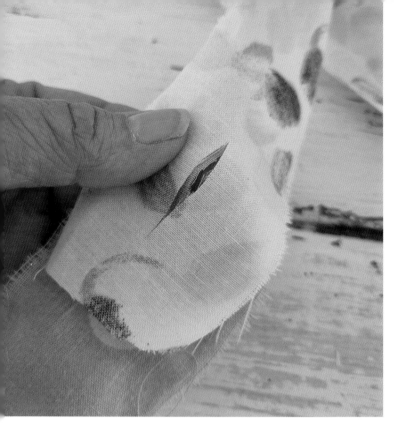

14. Line the two strips up with the new strip on top and facing away from you.

15. Keeping the two pieces pinched together, take the top strip and push it through both slits from below.

16. Gently pull through until the two lengths are joined, then continue to work as before.

17. If the mat does look a tiny bit 'pancakey' as you work, don't panic! The stitches are very forgiving so you will find that as you walk on the finished rug it should flatten out beautifully.

ELDERFLOWER CORDIAL

The heady floral fragrance of elderflowers is one of highlights of early summer, as throughout late May and early June the creamy white blossoms grace hedgerows and footpaths. This glorious cordial is so easy to make, and will add a beautiful floral note to your recipes. Serve with sparkling water and ice on a hot day, use as a base for a cracking cocktail or add to prosecco for a special lunch in the garden. Mixed with icing sugar it tastes delicious as a frosting on cakes and biscuits, or spoon over a warm lemon drizzle cake for extra flavour; it can also be added to jams and jellies, poured over ice cream or even whipped into cream for a summery pavlova.

Ingredients

- 25 elderflower heads
- 1kg granulated white sugar
- 1.5 litres water
- 3 unwaxed oranges, roughly chopped
- 2 unwaxed lemons, roughly chopped
- 50g citric acid
- Sterilised glass bottles

Method

1. Pick the elderflowers on a sunny morning, after the dew has evaporated.

2. Don't wash the heads, just give them a vigorous shake to remove any bugs; I often leave the blossom spread out on a tea towel for half an hour just to let the little blighters escape. Cut off the thick stem as close as possible to the flowers, as it can make the syrup bitter.

3. Tip the sugar into a large ceramic bowl then pour over 1.5l of boiling water and stir so the sugar starts to dissolve.

4. Allow to cool, then add the chopped fruit, citric acid and flower heads. Give everything a final stir then cover with a clean tea towel.

5. Steep the mixture for 48 hours, stirring occasionally, before straining through a sieve lined with scalded muslin. Pour into sterilised bottles and store in the fridge where it will keep for a good six weeks.

6. If you are making a large batch, it can be poured into sterilised plastic containers and frozen so you have a supply all summer; we always freeze some in ice cube trays to pop in cold drinks (most notably gin and tonic!).

Summer

HOW TO DRY FLOWER PETALS

Dried flower petals are a useful supply to keep in your craft cupboard, as they add a lovely touch of colour and rustic feel to so many projects. From home-made paper to bath salts, and soap to confetti, a sprinkling of petals always feels like a little gift from nature. Daisies, hydrangeas, delphiniums, lavender, roses and marigolds (calendula) all dry beautifully, but there are a few simple tips to remember which will guarantee success.

1. Only pick flowers which you know have not been sprayed with any chemicals, particularly if you wish to use them for home-made bath products or as a cooking ingredient or garnish. Avoid drying petals from florists or supermarkets for this reason as they will have been treated with pesticides.

2. Pick the flowers on a dry morning after the dew has evaporated, then remove the petals and spread them out in a single layer on kitchen paper on wire racks (they can sometimes stick together so try and space them evenly). Either leave them under a hot sun or pop them in the airing cupboard with plenty of room for air to circulate for a few days until they are dry and crispy. Store in an airtight container, ideally in a cool, dark place.

3. If you only need a few petals for a craft project and are in a hurry, lay them on a plate covered in kitchen paper, then place another sheet of kitchen roll on top and pop them in the microwave. As each microwave varies in efficiency the time it takes for them to dry will differ, so experiment by giving them thirty-second blasts.

4. If the petals get wet the colours may bleed, so be warned (just in case you plan to throw them at a beautiful bride in a white dress on a wet day).

5. Long a symbol of love, and famed for their heady fragrance, roses are best picked when they are still slightly furled and less likely to have brown areas on the petals; even a small patch can turn the whole petal brown so these are best avoided. Red or pink blooms give a much more attractive appearance than cream or white roses, which may end up as a fairly uninspiring beige.

6. Dried rose petals can be made into tea to help digestive ailments or ease menstrual cramps and menopause symptoms. Use the petals to garnish summer cakes or as an ingredient for home-made bath bombs, soaps and face masks, where its antioxidant properties will ease tired or reddened skin. You can also make a simple syrup by bringing 1 cup of water, ½ cup of dried rose petals and 1 cup of sugar to the boil; simmer for 10 minutes, allow to cool and then strain. It will keep for up to two weeks in the fridge or can be frozen, and adds a lovely summery touch to party cocktails.

7. Lavender should be harvested before it flowers, and can either be left whole on the stem or the buds stripped off to give you that lovely lilac rice grain effect. Stitch into little bags to scent your wardrobe or pop under your pillow to ease you into a restful sleep; the intoxicating scent is also said to alleviate headaches and migraines.

8. Marigold, or calendula as it is often known, has gloriously sunny coloured petals that retain a strongly happy hue when dried. As such, they are perfect for paper making, but they can also be made into a herbal tea (calendula has excellent anti-inflammatory properties so is a splendid way to soothe a sore throat). Used in home-made bath preparations, they do a super job at easing skin irritation.

ROSE PETAL AND OAT MILK BATH

There are few things more pleasurable after a long day in the garden than plunging into a warm bath, especially when it is packed full of nourishing ingredients to moisturise that outdoor skin.

Beloved of Cleopatra, and Nero's wife, Poppaea Sabina, milk baths are particularly beneficial to dry bodies as the lactic acid acts as a natural exfoliant. Although they both loved asses' milk, here we are using dried cow's milk as it is freely available in most supermarkets. Other ingredients can be mixed and matched depending on what you have in the cupboard, and although I have used lavender and frankincense essential oils, please feel free to play

with your fragrance! Just remember not to exceed the recommended dose of drops and only use skin-safe oils; neroli, geranium, ylang ylang and chamomile all have not only fabulous scents but skincare benefits too.

Usually I like my oats in a porridge, but they are also well known for their moisturising properties and have long been used as a treatment for eczema and itchy skin. Other additions can include bicarbonate of soda which is naturally antiseptic and softening, while cornflour adds a delightful silkiness to the water. Rose petals are the final touch and lend a pretty pink texture to the mix.

One of the issues with a bath filled with petals or other additions is that they can lead to a clogged plug hole, so as we don't want to undo all that dreamy bath time relaxation by having to go and find a sink plunger afterwards, the rose petals and oats are whizzed in a food processor to minimise tedious clean-up. I keep pretty jam jars all year round then make a big batch to fill them as gifts; add half to one cupful to a warm bath, sink back and relax.

Ingredients

- 1 cup dried full fat milk powder (coconut milk powder makes a great alternative)
- 1 cup porridge oats
- ½ cup baking soda
- ½ cup cornflour
- ½ cup dried rose petals (about a handful)
- 15 drops skin-safe essential oils; I used 7 drops frankincense and 8 of lavender

Method

1. Place the rose petals and oats in a blender and whizz until ground.

2. Tip the mixture into a large ceramic bowl and add the other dry ingredients.

3. Sprinkle over the essential oils and stir thoroughly until fully blended, before packing into glass jars and adding a pretty label.

4. Leave for 24 hours for the essential oils to infuse before use.

MUM'S FAVOURITE PERSIAN LOVE CAKE

Imagine if you will, the heady promise of a traditional lemon drizzle cake taken to new exotic heights with fragrant Middle Eastern flavours and spices, then decorated with some of your beautiful dried rose petals; perfect for a special afternoon tea or summer celebration. A moist almond, cardamom and pistachio cake is lightly drenched with lemon and rosewater syrup while still warm, then spread with a zesty lemon icing. This is what my mother insists

on calling 'a proper icing', none of that fluffy, buttery stuff that the rest of us could eat all evening with a spoon. She says it tastes even better on the second day, when all the beautiful flavours really start to shine through.

A word about rosewater; rather than buying it in the baking section of your local supermarket, have a look in the World Foods aisle, where it seems to be about a third of the price. Secondly, different brands can vary wildly in strength. If in doubt, go easy with it, as our hope is the cake will evoke the heady scent of a warm summer's day, rather than a bottle of complimentary hotel shampoo.

Ingredients

For the cake
- 110g butter, softened
- 150g caster sugar
- 250g ground almonds
- 180g self-raising flour
- 4 eggs
- 2 large tablespoons Greek yoghurt
- 10 cardamom pods
- Zest and juice of one lemon
- 1 tablespoon rosewater
- 25g green pistachio kernels, chopped

For the drizzle
- 2 tablespoons caster sugar
- Juice of half a lemon
- 1 teaspoon rosewater

For the icing
- 150g icing sugar
- Juice of half a lemon
- 25g green pistachio kernels, chopped
- Edible dried rose petals

Method

1. Preheat your oven to 175°C. Grease and line a 20cm baking tin with greaseproof paper.

2. Using a pestle and mortar, crush the cardamom pods until the shells split. Remove the husks and then grind the seeds that are left behind until they begin to release their wonderful floral fragrance.

3. Using either a stand mixer or an electric whisk, beat together the butter and sugar until they are light and fluffy.

4. Add the eggs one by one, accompanying each with a hefty spoonful of flour to stop the mixture curdling.

5. Tip in the rest of the flour, ground almonds, yoghurt, lemon juice, zest and rosewater and mix again until thoroughly combined.

6. Lastly, stir in the chopped pistachios and scrape into your prepared tin. Bake for 40–45 minutes in the centre of the oven or until a poked-in skewer comes out clean (I tend to check it after about 35 minutes and then pop a piece of tinfoil over the top if it looks as though it is browning too quickly).

7. As soon as you have removed the cake from the oven, place the ingredients for the drizzle in a small pan and set over a medium heat. Bring to a simmer and stir until all the sugar has dissolved.

8. Carefully tip the still-warm cake out on to a wire rack and peel off the greaseproof paper (the top is now essentially the bottom, giving you a lovely flat surface to ice). Poke lots of little holes all over the cake with a cocktail stick then slowly pour over the drizzle.

9. Once the cake is completely cold, prepare the icing. Sieve the icing sugar into a large bowl and then stir in the lemon juice. Keep adding drops of cold water, a few at a time, until you have a thick icing. Tip it into the middle of the cake, then gently encourage it out towards the sides using the back of a spoon.

10. Sprinkle over the chopped pistachios and dried rose petals.

VINTAGE CAKE STAND

A summer tea party is a wonderful way to celebrate a special occasion, and this vintage cake stand will add a lovely retro twist when used to display your tiny sandwiches and sweet treats. I have a particular fondness for buying blue and white china whenever I see it at jumble sales or in charity shops, so a quick rifle in my kitchen cupboards provided an assortment of mismatched family and foraged crockery for these projects; perfect for a birthday tea or DIY wedding!

Drilling ceramics for the first time can be slightly daunting, so I would suggest initially practising on a less-loved piece, just so you can feel how the drill bit bites into the china. Some plates are also

much denser than others so the time taken to drill through can vary considerably; don't panic and apply too much pressure, just let the drill do the work, as my grandfather would say. It is also terribly important that you only use a cordless battery drill as we will be using water and it doesn't mix well with electricity.

Materials

- A small, medium and large vintage plate (plus optional teacup)
- Battery-powered drill

- 6mm drill bit for tiles and ceramics
- 3-tier cake stand fittings (readily available online)
- Marker pen
- Masking tape
- Safety glasses
- Bowl of water and a sponge
- Old towel
- Hot glue gun and glue sticks

Method

1. To drill your first hole, first apply a couple of pieces of masking tape to the centre of both sides of the plate. (It won't stay on long but should help stop the glaze from chipping; it also means the drill bit won't slip all over the place, just for the first few seconds.) Find the centre of the plate using a tape measure and mark with a pen.

2. The hole should only be a tiny bit larger than the cake stand fittings so double check the measurements before you start (the majority available online seem to work perfectly with a 6mm bit).

3. Fold the towel up to make a non-slip base for your work and put on the safety glasses, just in case there is the odd chip of flying glaze.

4. Place the plate face up on the towel and drip a little water on to the centre of the plate. Hold the drill at right angles to the plate and begin to drill slowly, just applying the smallest pressure. The faster the bit turns the greater the chance of the ceramic chipping, so take it easy to start with.

5. As the bit starts to bite, keep sponging more water on to the centre of the plate so the drill tip is always wet. This not only reduces the dust in the air but also helps keep it cool.

6. As the hole gets deeper, wiggle the drill around a bit to make it larger.

7. You will know you have reached the other side when all the water suddenly disappears. Flip the plate over, add a little more water and gently drill again until the hole is a consistent width all the way

through (you may get a few little chips on this side but they will be covered by a washer).

8. Repeat with the other two plates before washing and drying them thoroughly.

9. To assemble the stand, first put a metal washer then a plastic one over the bolt before pushing it up through the largest plate from underneath.

10. Put a plastic washer over the bolt and then screw on one of the long poles, tightening it up from underneath with a screwdriver if necessary.

11. Repeat with the next plate. The order is always the same; metal washer, plastic washer, plate, plastic washer, pole; essentially you are making a plastic sandwich to protect the plate while keeping the cake stand together.

12. Finally, add the top ring. If the rim around the base plate is shallower than the bolt and washer it might be a little wobbly and unstable when you put the stand on a flat surface. This is easily fixed by heating up your glue gun and adding three or four blobs of hot glue to make little feet (although if you find this a necessary step the

bottom plate will have to be washed by hand rather than bunged in the dishwasher).

13. The cake stand can easily be taken apart for storage; I drilled a hole through the bottom of a teacup and sometimes add this to the stand for serving sweeties or tiny treats if there are children at the party!

UPCYCLED SUITCASE PICNIC TABLE

Whenever I am feeling under the weather, I have an overwhelming compulsion to scroll through auction websites browsing vintage suitcases, and thus I have a large stack of them gathering dust in the corner of my bedroom, accumulated over many years. Friends and family also stockpile those pretty gingham jam jars for me; they make a great way of transporting picnic foods such as salad, dips and sweeties, while tiny jars are ideal for condiments, jam for

scones, salad dressing and salt and pepper. After a few hours of assessing my craft stash followed by a little sawing and gluing, the result was this retro suitcase picnic set.

Wooden or hardshell cases are perfect for this project, as legs can be attached to the base to make a handy little picnic table and then removed and stored neatly inside when not in use. It is not a lightweight option for picnicking, I grant you, but for camping, country fairs or the races it makes a lovely set up! The champagne

flutes and vintage crockery were picked up for a couple of pounds from local charity shops, while the legs are easy to source online.

I think it would also make an unusual coffee table or sewing box, or even a kid's activity table for camping, filled with paints, pens, games and sketch books. While I was making the picnic table I also knocked up a little case to keep all my most useful crafty bits and pieces together. The pin cushion is made from a jam jar lid, and both this and the storage tins and notebook are held on to the lid with self-adhesive hook and loop dots. A snack tube was covered in vintage fabric for pliers and craft knives, and jam jars make the perfect container for buttons and beads.

Materials

(Not an exhaustive list of materials, do please feel free to improvise with whatever you have in your craft cupboard)
- Hardshell or wooden suitcase
- Set of four 25cm beech wooden table legs with fixing plates and screws
- 8mm particle board or similar (ply or chipboard would work equally well)
- 50mm metal corner protectors (if necessary) plus screws
- Drill and drill bit
- Screwdriver
- Jigsaw
- Staple gun and staples
- Spray adhesive
- Hot glue gun
- Chalk paint
- Clear furniture wax
- Ribbon
- Cotton/polyester fabric (the blue and white gingham was left over from my kitchen curtains)
- 6mm elastic
- Vintage crockery, champagne flutes and jam jars

Method

1. Clean the suitcase thoroughly, removing all paper and fabric lining. Often the odd odour may linger, in which case spraying the case with white vinegar and leaving it in the sun to dry should help. If smells persist, fill a saucer with bicarbonate of soda, pop inside, close the lid and leave for a few days and this should do the trick.

2. If the suitcase corners look a little tatty, drill pilot holes in the case and then screw on the corner brackets to cover them.

3. Apply two coats of chalk paint and allow to dry.

4. Using a soft cloth, rub over a thin layer of clear furniture wax to protect the paint, and buff gently.

5. As we will be screwing legs into the base and using a staple gun inside the lid, both will need lining with particle board so the hardware doesn't poke through into the suitcase.

6. Cut two pieces of board, one for the lid and one for the base, ensuring they are a couple of millimetres smaller than the case to

allow for the fabric lining. If your suitcase is the clamshell type, there will be plenty of room for it to close properly; if it is an envelope type of lid, you may need to cut them fractionally smaller so that you will be able to shut it.

7. Cut four pieces of card to fit the sides and back of the base of the case.

8. Cut three sections from the hardboard to make the dividers; they should be a couple of millimetres shorter and narrower than the case to allow for the fabric covering.

9. Press your fabric if necessary, and following the manufacturer's instructions, spray the base, lid, dividers and card with adhesive and then smooth over the fabric. (Leave the spray adhesive for a few seconds once you have applied it, otherwise you may end up with a wet looking patch on the fabric.)

10. Using the hot glue gun, attach the two sections of hardboard to the lid and base, before sticking in the cardboard sides and back.

11. Fix in the dividers, then glue some pretty ribbon around the edges of the case to cover any unsightly joins.

12. Close the case and turn it over. Drill holes for the fixing plates on to the base and screw them on tightly, making sure that when the legs are attached they are angled towards the corners; the screws need to be shorter than the thickness of the case and the base lining combined, so if necessary use smaller ones than those provided.

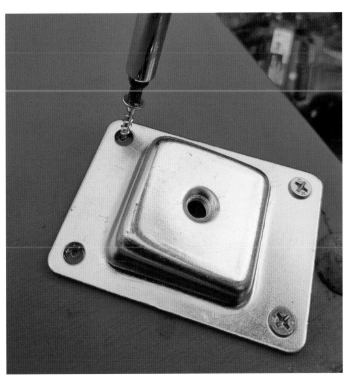

13. Open the case back up and lay it down so the lid is lying flat on your work surface. To attach the first tea plate, snip two pieces of elastic the same width as the plate. Fix to the lid at an angle of 45 degrees by tucking 2cm under at each end and stapling in place. I would staple it a couple of times, just to make sure the elastic doesn't ping off as soon as you put the plate in! Repeat with the other piece to make a cross shape. Make three more elastic crosses to hold the other plates.

14. To attach the little jars, take a piece of elastic roughly twice the length of the jars and staple the first 2cm on to the suitcase lid (with the long end stretching away from where the jars will be fixed). Hold your first jar in place and bring the elastic over the top, stretching it a little before stapling in place. Repeat with two more jars before trimming the elastic and finishing with another 2cm tucked under section.

15. I had to be a little more creative in my approach to the champagne glasses, and just fiddled around to see what worked! I measured the diameter at the top and middle of the glass and cut two pieces of elastic to size, before tucking 2cm under at each end in a hoop shape, and stapling on, as before.

16. Place your other bits and pieces inside the case and work out where you would like your dividers to go before fixing them in position with the hot glue gun; if any items stored in the lid protrude (like the champagne glasses), you may need to juggle things around to ensure that the suitcase will close.

17. I also found a vintage bottle opener, so simply stapled a length of ribbon into the lid and tied the opener in place with a bow.

WILDFLOWER SUMMER CANDLES

I think most people will have memories of pressing flowers as a child, and there is something very calming about letting your eyes wander over green fields and verges looking for specimens to preserve. Wildflowers (or 'weeds' as they were popularly known when we were kids) are ideal for picking on a warm summer's day; while you can speed the process up by pressing them between sheets of greaseproof paper under a warm iron, I infinitely prefer the old-fashioned method of tucking them in between the pages of an old book and periodically checking on them. Patience is part of the pleasure (although my friends will laugh when they read this as I tend to check them every 20 minutes, having all the patience of a toddler in a bakery).

Materials

- Old books
- Sheets of scrap copy paper
- A selection of flowers and leaves
- A pillar candle
- Adhesive spray or PVA glue
- Greaseproof paper
- Sticky tape
- An iron

Method

1. Choose your flowers and foliage; ideally you are looking for something with a single layer of petals/leaves. Meadow buttercups (Ranunculus acris), small daisies (Bellis perennis), cranesbill (Geranium pratense) and ferns are all prolific in summer and perfect for pressing.

2. As usual, pick them on a warm sunny morning so they are good and dry.

3. Place the leaves and flowers in a single layer between two sheets of scrap copy paper and then slip between the leaves of a large book. (The pages of the book may wrinkle as the moisture from the flowers

evaporates, so don't use your most valuable first edition leather-bound Arthur Conan Doyle.)

4. Weigh the book down, either with a stack of hardbacks or something equally heavy. Leave for 3–4 weeks until all the blooms and foliage are completely dry.

5. Lay the pressed flowers out until you are happy with your design,

then give them a light mist of spray adhesive (or a dab of PVA glue). They will be very fragile, so using great care (and possibly some tweezers) apply them on to the candle and gently pat down in place.

6. Cut a piece of greaseproof paper large enough to cover the sides of the candle and tape tightly around it using the sticky tape.

7. Make sure there is no water in your iron (we are trying to avoid moisture) and heat it to the 'low' setting. Minding your fingers, gently rub the iron over the surface of the greaseproof paper in tiny circular movements; as the wax melts you will see the colour change slightly as the pressed flowers become embedded in the candle. (Don't be tempted to rush things by having the iron too hot; the flowers may get dragged across the surface of the candle and the colours may bleed. In addition, you might find the odd

drip of molten wax leaks unseen from the bottom of the candle all over your favourite skirt.)

8. Once you have ironed all the pressed material, carefully remove the paper and check everything has stuck fast; if any areas need a little more heat, just tape the paper back over and apply the iron once more.

9. Remove the paper, place the candle on a suitable heat-resistant surface and trim the wick to around 5mm to ensure an even burn and clean flame. As ever, please keep all burning candles away from draughts, kids, pets and curtains; the pressed flowers will burn away with the wax but any excess or loose pieces should be removed before re-lighting.

MINI LAMPSHADE FAIRY LIGHTS

Whether dining outside at midsummer or planning a family camping weekend, a little extra light is always welcome on summer evenings; these dinky little lampshade fairy lights will add some vintage charm for when you are tripping over guy ropes in the dark. A rummage in my recycling bin provided all sorts of interesting possibilities for this project; the plastic vessels used include (but were not limited to) yoghurt pots, hand sanitiser, Indian takeaway mango chutney pots, balsamic vinegar salad dressing and a bottle of utterly over-priced organic shampoo.

When picking your bottles, aim for those that have a little bit of squish to them as the more rigid ones can crack when you attempt to make a hole. Here I have used a drill but you could also use a pyrography tool to melt them; if so, I would do it outside because of the fumes, and also throw the pyrography tip away afterwards as it will be covered in molten plastic.

Materials
- Battery operated fairy lights, with 10 bulbs
- An assortment of clear plastic bottles, pudding pots and containers

- Fabric scraps, ribbon, ric-rac and trims (a pretty patchwork pillow case provided ample material for this project)
- PVA glue
- Paint brush
- Hot glue gun
- Drill and 6mm drill bit
- Craft knife

Method

1. Prepare the bottles by washing and drying them thoroughly. Any sticky residue left by labels can be removed by making a paste with bicarbonate of soda and a few drops of vegetable oil. Smear the paste over the glue and leave for a few minutes; the adhesive should then scrub off quite easily with a pan scourer in hot soapy water.

2. Using the craft knife, trim off any rims on the pudding pots. Cut the bottles down to the size you would like; I find the easiest way to make the cut vaguely straight is by holding a tape measure around the bottle then drawing along the line with a marker pen.

3. Drill holes in the bottom of each plastic bottle using a bit slightly larger than the fairy light bulb; a 6mm bit seems to do the job

admirably. (Don't apply too much pressure initially, just in case the plastic is tempted to crack.)

4. At first, I thought I was going to have to make a paper pattern for each little lampshade but quickly realised there was a far lazier (sorry, more efficient) way of doing it. Cut a piece of fabric large enough to wrap round the shade, and with a couple of centimetres excess all round.

5. Dilute the PVA 3 to 1 with water and brush all over the lampshade.

6. Place the shade on one end of the fabric and roll along it until the shape is covered, smoothing out any bubbles as you go.

7. Trim the excess fabric so you are left with a neat 1cm overlap, then apply some more glue to this edge and smooth it on to the bottle. If the bottle has a nice flat bottom, as it were, it will be very easy to roll it in the fabric; for the more rounded bottom, once the material has been soaked in glue for a few moments it will have a little stretch, so you can pull it tight over any curves.

8. Check again for any air bubbles and push them out with your fingers, then allow the fabric to dry completely.

9. Using sharp fabric scissors, trim the top and bottom of the lampshade.

10. Glue trim and ribbon to the top and bottom to cover the fabric seams using the hot glue gun; pom-pom trim looks beautiful hanging from the lower edge, and ric-rac works very well at the top seam as it is easy to bend in a circle. Lay the lampshades out in the order you would like them, then poke a light bulb through each hole in the top.

11. Finally add a blob of glue to the cable where it enters the lampshades in order to fix the fairy lights in place.

BOHO BEACH BAG

I don't know about you, but I never seem to have enough bags in the car, whether it be for a quick trip to the shops or a day on the beach, so these fabulous totes are ideal for keeping in the glove box. Made from old T-shirts, the bags can be fashioned in just 5 minutes.

Kids' shirts are the perfect size for produce bags, whereas larger sizes are ideally suited for all the clobber needed for a day at the seaside; they are brilliant for wet swimming suits as you can just throw the whole lot in the washing machine at the end of the day. The bags are knotted at the bottom edge, so you can either leave the tassels hanging down for a boho look, or turn the shirt inside out before you start so the knots will ultimately be hidden.

Materials (to make a tasselled bag)

- Crew neck T-shirt or a sleeveless vest (the latter are ideal as they come ready made with handles)
- Sharp fabric scissors
- A tea plate
- 12mm wooden beads with 5mm hole
- Large-eyed darning needle

Method

1. Lay your T-shirt on a flat surface and using a plate as a guide, cut round the neck to make the top of the bag.

2. Cut off both sleeves just inside the seam.

3. Snip along the bottom hem of the T-shirt at intervals of about 2cm; I wanted quite a long fringe on this bag so the cuts were roughly 10cm deep, but if you wanted to hide the knots inside then about 5cm should be sufficient.

4. Starting at one end, tie the opposing strips together to form a knot (pull the knot nice and tight so you don't end up with gaps in the bottom of your bag) then repeat all the way to the end to make the fringe.

5. Thread the first tassel on to the darning needle and push through one of the wooden beads. Tie a knot in the end to keep the bead in place, then repeat with the rest of the fringe; this shirt measured roughly 45cm across, so with tassels measuring 2cm in width I used forty-four beads.

6. If you prefer a bag with a plainer bottom, turn the shirt inside out before you knot it, then trim the tassels off; when you turn back the right way out all the knots should be hidden.

GIANT BUBBLE MIX

The cooler days of late summer are the perfect time of year for blowing giant bubbles; not too much scorching sun, not too windy and the air is becoming damp, so get outside with the kids and enjoy the last of the good weather! Early morning or evening is best for giant bubbles as the moisture in the air will stop them popping too quickly. The more bubbles you make, the better they get too; as the string becomes saturated you will find it much easier to get the mixture to stay on the wands.

This mix is easily made with a few store cupboard ingredients. I would add that a) I have found traditional green Fairy liquid the best detergent to use, and b) buying the glycerine in bulk from the chemist or online is much cheaper than the supermarket baking aisle. (It can be used as a treatment for sore throats and coughs and is a moisturising ingredient in many home-made beauty products; add a teaspoon per 100g of flour in your cake recipes and it will keep the crumbs moist for longer too.)

Once you have made the liquid, let it settle for at least an hour before using; overnight it is even better. Plastic lidded boxes or buckets are the ideal container for the mixture so it can be taken camping or on picnics; I found ours at a local ice cream parlour, who always seem more than happy to give them away.

Materials

For the bubble mix
- 6 cups of tap water
- ½ cup of washing up liquid
- ½ cup of cornflour
- 1 tablespoon baking powder
- 1 tablespoon glycerine

For the wands
- 1 x 6ft bamboo garden cane
- Hot glue gun
- 2 metal screw eyes
- A metal washer
- Cotton yarn or string

Method

1. Place the water, washing up liquid, cornflour, baking powder and glycerine together in a bucket or washing up bowl, stirring gently

until the cornflour dissolves. Try not to agitate it too much as little bubbles in the mix won't help you make big bubbles.

2. Next, make your wands. Cut the bamboo cane in half, then screw an eyelet into the top of each one. Add a blob of hot glue to fix it securely if necessary.

3. Cut two thick cotton yarns or strings, one measuring 90cm, and the other 200cm.

4. Tie the short piece between the two eyelets.

5. Tie one end of the longer length on to the first bamboo stick, thread on a washer and then tie the string on to the second stick. Having a washer or nut at the bottom of this longer string not only makes it easier to dip in the mixture, it also keeps the line weighted nicely when you are creating huge bubble tubes.

6. To make a bubble, hold both sticks together and gently lower the string into the mixture until it is soaked through. Lift it back out and carefully pull the sticks apart. As the breeze catches the mix it will start to make a tube (standing with your back to the wind will help fill it naturally). Simply move the wands back together to close the bubble off then watch it float away.

Autumn

LAZY HARVEST BUTTER

Increased porridge consumption is a sign the weather is definitely getting colder, and a spoonful of this unctuous spiced fruit puree will add a welcome touch of autumnal cheer to your breakfast. At its heart, it is basically a stewed apple recipe, but cooked over a period of long hours so the fruit caramelises and turns a gorgeous dark brown. While it can be made on the hob, there is a definite appeal to just chucking everything in the slow cooker first thing in the morning, and leaving it to its own devices, rather than having to constantly stir for 2 hours. The other brilliant thing is that the fruit does not need to be peeled laboriously, you can just roughly hack the cores out.

Fruit butters don't actually contain any butter at all, the name actually refers to their spreadable consistency. Popular in the Netherlands, Belgium and Germany since the Middle Ages, where monks would make apple butter using fruit from monastery orchards, the tradition then spread across the Atlantic with the Pennsylvania Dutch. However, as I like to throw in whatever I can beg, borrow or scrump, this

recipe also contains blackberries and pears; if you have any plums left, pop them in too.

Containing much less sugar than a traditional jam it is not a preserve as such. Divide the cooked mixture so you have one portion for the fridge, where it will keep happily for up to two weeks, then split the rest between containers or ziplock bags and freeze. It will store well, frozen, for up to a year so you can just defrost some as and when you fancy. Spoon over porridge or yoghurt, spread over fresh bread or serve with pancakes; it also makes delicious little puff pastry turnovers or as an accompaniment to roast pork.

This will take a large 6-litre slow cooker to fit in everything, so if yours is smaller, the ingredients are easily halved.

Ingredients

- 2.5kg of fruit, such as apples, pears and blackberries (I used 1.5kg of apples, 1kg of pears and then threw in 100g of blackberries for good measure. If you prefer a less grainy texture, add fewer pears, or omit them altogether)
- 150g brown sugar
- 150g white sugar
- Zest of 1 lemon
- Juice of half a lemon
- 2 heaped teaspoons of ground cinnamon
- ½ teaspoon allspice
- 4 cloves
- 1 teaspoon vanilla essence

Method (takes 12 hours)

Prepare the fruit by quartering the apples and pears and removing the cores and pips. Chop roughly (and I do mean roughly, this is a lazy recipe after all), and place in the slow cooker.

1. Grind the cloves to a powder in a pestle and mortar, remove any tough woody stalks and tip over the fruit.

2. Add the blackberries, sugar, lemon juice, zest and spices, give everything a good stir and then set your slow cooker to the 'low' setting.

3. Cook for 7–8 hours, stirring occasionally to break up the fruit. When the fruit has collapsed, either blend the mixture to a puree by using a stick blender, or whizz it all in batches in a food processor and then return it to the crockpot and continue to cook.

4. After 10 hours, check the flavour, adding more cinnamon and sugar if you like (you may need a little extra sweetness if your apples were very tart). I made one batch with eight cloves and it had distinctly medicinal overtones, so less is more with that one!

5. Reset the timer for another 2 hours, but this time prop the lid open with a couple of wooden spoons to allow the moisture to escape and the mixture to thicken up.

6. Once the slow cooker pings again, stir through the vanilla essence and allow to cool slightly before potting into a sterilised glass jar. Bag or box the rest up and store in the freezer until required.

ACORN TOADSTOOL GARLAND

This garland was inspired by a potter round outside on a sunny but wild and windy afternoon. We have three huge oak trees in our garden, and as soon as the autumn winds pick up in late September or October there is a very real chance of being struck on the back of the head by flying acorns. As the acorns come hurtling

through the air, fly agaric toadstools (*Amanita muscaria*) are popping up in the damp woodlands nearby. Long associated with fairies, the highly toxic fungi are so called because tiny pieces used to be floated in a bowl of milk to repel flies.

Acorns meanwhile have long been a feature of mythology in Northern Europe. Oaks, as one of the tallest specimens in the forest (and with a high moisture content) are said to attract lightning, so the trees naturally became associated with Thor, the Norse god of thunder. In traditional folklore, a bowl of acorns placed on your window ledge would thus protect your home from lightning. With some preparation to remove their toxic tannins they are edible, but using them for a Sunday afternoon craft seems much more fun than laboriously processing them to make a rather grim coffee substitute.

Materials (to make 1.5-metre garland)

- 12 acorns (definitely bake extra just in case!)
- 8mm jump or split rings
- White chalk paint
- Red acrylic paint
- Jute string
- 10 tiny bells (roughly 10mm in diameter)
- Matt spray varnish
- Hot glue gun and glue
- Pliers or tweezers
- Wooden cocktail or kebab stick

Method

1. To ensure there are no nasty little wiggly surprises living inside your beautiful acorns they first need to be cleaned and prepared thoroughly. Harvest them as soon as they fall from the tree (you need to beat the squirrels), and discard any that have obvious holes

or damage. Wash in warm soapy water, scrubbing away any soil or leaf litter, before allowing them to dry thoroughly.

2. Snap off any stalks, then remove the caps. (As acorns dry out, the caps do tend to fall off; for this project we are removing them anyway, but I would suggest that whatever craft idea you have in mind, remove the little hats and then stick them back on using adhesive just so you know they are secure.)

3. Preheat your oven to 100°C. Line a baking sheet with tinfoil and spread the acorns out in a single layer (don't worry if there are any green areas as these will turn a lovely nutty brown colour as they dry out). Bake them for around 2–3 hours, shaking the tray occasionally to turn them and let any moisture escape the oven. Allow to cool in the oven, leaving the door slightly ajar.

4. Squeeze a little hot glue from the end of the gun nozzle. Dip a jump ring in the adhesive using either pliers or tweezers before quickly blobbing the ring on to an acorn cap and holding it in place until secure. Pull away any wispy threads of glue. (If you don't have any jump rings handy, you can cut 1.5cm of 0.8mm wire and bend it into a loop as an alternative.)

5. Paint both the caps and rings with white chalk paint; this gives, subsequently, a much brighter shade of red, and also gives a slightly smoother surface on which to paint the dots. I like to put the cap on the end of my finger like a little hat in order to coat it all the way round before lifting it off with a wooden kebab stick.

6. Allow to dry, then paint the caps with red acrylic craft paint (two coats will give a lovely bright colour).

7. Once they are completely dry, add spots of white paint to give the appearance of little toadstools. With my caffeine-shaky hands, I find the end of a cocktail stick gives a much neater blob than using a brush.

8. Allow to dry once again before giving both the caps and acorns a couple of coats of matt varnish to protect them and make them last longer.

9. If the holes on the bells are too small to pass the string through, you may need to attach a jump ring to each one using pliers.

10. Heat the hot glue gun up once again and add a generous blob of adhesive to the pointy end of each acorn before fixing into the painted cap.

11. Cut a 160cm length of string. Leave the first 25cm free, then starting with an acorn, thread them alternately with the bells at intervals of about 5cm.

12. Tie a hanging loop on to each end.

13. Any extra toadstools can be hung on to twine and used to decorate your festive tree or used to decorate special gifts.

HEDGEROW SCHNAPPS

When autumn sees an abundance of berries in the hedges and fields, hedgerow schnapps is the obvious (and cheap!) answer, made with wonderful seasonal fruit such as hawthorn berries, sloes, blackberries and crab apples.

Some words of caution: make sure you identify the berries correctly, as there are some poisonous yet enticingly pretty ones draped through the undergrowth, such as bryony. This grows on a vine rather than a tree so is easily identified; just keep an eye on the kids and

make sure they don't pick anything unless you've checked it.

Young hawthorn shoots can be eaten raw in spring (they used to be known as 'bread and cheese' and taste rather like a budget lettuce); while the flesh of the hawthorn berries is safe to consume and is good for sore throats, the seeds are poisonous so must never be swallowed. Sloes are so astringent that if you eat one raw it makes your face feel as though it has turned inside out, and the fluffy white stuff inside rosehips is also a skin irritant (and used to be used as a budget itching powder, so my grandfather told me) so leave the hips whole. Don't let me put you off trying this recipe though, as the resulting drink is smooth, fragrant and makes a fabulous after dinner liqueur. Crab apples make a lovely addition too, washed, cored and cut into chunks; you can leave the skin on to reduce any unnecessary

faffing. If I have any squishy raspberries lurking in the fridge during the infusing period I always throw those in as well.

Ingredient
- 1 litre vodka (supermarket own brand is fine)
- 500g mixed berries and fruit (in this case, 250g blackberries (Rubus fruticosus), 50g sloes (Prunus spinosa), 50g rosehips (Rosa canina), 50g haws (Crataegus monogyna), and a handful of crab apples (Malus sylvestris)
- 250g sugar

Method
1. Prepare your berries. I used blackberries as the main bulk, and these just need a quick wash. Remove any stalks from the haws, then rinse along with the sloes and rosehips. Sloes are best picked after the first frost, but as the devil supposedly spits on blackberries on 29 September you shouldn't pick them after this, picking the sloes and rosehips early and popping them in the freezer overnight will have the same effect, helping the skins to soften and split.

2. Wash, quarter and core the little apples (if you can't find crab apples, pop in a dessert apple instead).

3. Sterilise a large 1.5 litre Kilner/Mason jar, either by warming it in the oven, or by putting it in the dishwasher on a hot cycle (lazy I know, but it seems to do the trick).

4. Layer the berries, apples and sugar in the clean jar, then top up with vodka.

5. Shake every day for seven days to dissolve the sugar, then store in a cool, dark cupboard for three months, before straining through a scalded muslin cloth and bottling. I tend to give it a little taste now and then, just to see if I need to adjust the sweetness and add more sugar.

6. Haws can cause a sediment if left for over a month, so if you are doing a purely hawthorn vodka I would strain it after four weeks then continue to store the liquid until it matures. However, just a handful doesn't seem to make the schnapps too murky if you do leave it for the full three months, and if it is a little cloudy you can always strain it through a coffee filter to clear it.

7. Keep in the freezer and drink in tiny glasses as a lovely winter evening treat!

STAMPED VINTAGE TEASPOON WINDCHIMES

As the autumn breezes start to pick up, these pretty windchimes will add some fun to your porch or decking as they tinkle away and alert you to the fact you really should bring the washing in. Made from vintage teaspoons, an old napkin ring and a broken necklace, they require few other materials and can easily be made in an evening. Stamp the spoons with names or dates for a charming anniversary or christening gift.

Materials
- Drill
- 2.5mm HSS drill bit (HSS stands for High Speed Steel and is ideal for drilling through light metals)
- Masking tape and pen
- Hammer and large nail
- A set of metal stamping alphabet punches
- Steel stamping hammer (optional)
- Bench block
- Round-nose or half-round pliers

- Wire cutters
- Safety goggles
- 3m roll of 8mm silver-plated copper wire
- Silver-plated napkin ring
- 4 vintage EPNS teaspoons
- A selection of glass beads
- 25mm split key ring

Method

1. Polish the spoons so they are a sparkling silver colour, using a metal polish if necessary.

2. Once you have decided on the words you wish to write, lay the letters out on your work surface the right way up; I have wrecked quite a few items by mistakenly stamping the last punch upside down, and it is not a happy feeling.

3. If you are stamping more than one line, it can be helpful to mark them out roughly with a felt tip. I also tend to stamp the middle letter of the word first as that helps to keep everything central.

4. Tutorials will often encourage you to tape the spoon to the stamping block, but not only does it add a huge layer of faff to the project, but with large flat spoons you can actually control the angle much more easily with your fingers. Hold the letter punch between your thumb and first finger and place it on the spoon, on top of the stamping block. Use your third and fourth fingers to angle the handle of the spoon so the bowl is flat against the work surface.

5. Give the head of the letter punch ten good smacks with the hammer; I would suggest that you sacrifice an extra spoon as a practice piece if it is your first time as the softness of cutlery can vary quite significantly

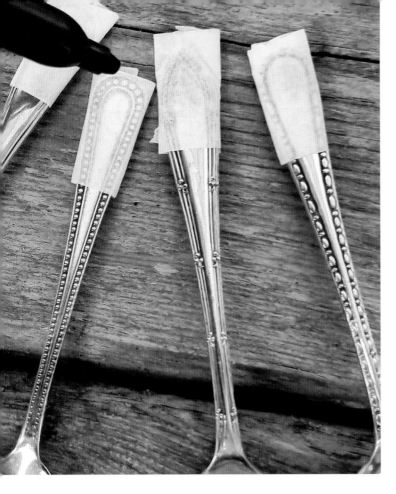

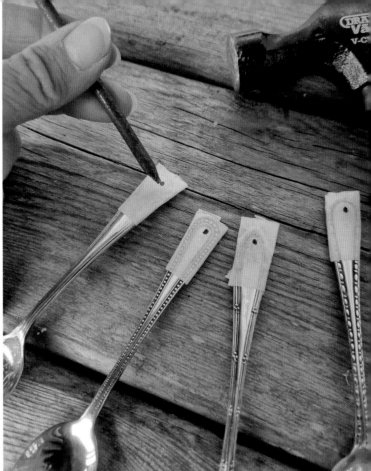

and you might find you need to give it a little more force. After the first couple of bangs the punch will start to engage with the metal and it is less likely to slip. Just remember that as they will be hanging with the bowl pointing downwards, the words will need to be the other way up so you can read them. At this stage you can colour over the script with a black marker pen before quickly wiping it off with a paper towel; this should help highlight the words nicely.

6. Wrap a little piece of masking tape around the handle of each spoon and mark with a dot where you would like the hanging hole to be (about 5mm from the end).

7. If you start drilling straight away there is a good chance the bit will slip about everywhere. To prevent this, take a large nail (5mm in this case), hold it firmly on the dot and give it ten to fifteen good hefty whacks with the hammer to make a pilot hole.

8. Put on your safety goggles. Place the teaspoon on a piece of scrap wood and drill through the spoon handle about 5mm from the end, pushing down firmly to stop the bit skidding. File off any rough edges, if indeed you have a metal file; the holes are so tiny that it's not really necessary if you haven't got one.

9. The napkin ring I used here conveniently already had holes in so I didn't need to worry about drilling any. However, if yours is a

solid ring, you will need to drill eight holes (four around the top and four around the bottom, at all points of the compass) in order for it to hang.

10. Cut eight 10cm, four 5cm and four 3.5cm lengths of wire using the wire cutters.

11. Take the pliers and make the four shortest pieces into an 'S' shape; grasp one end and bend it round to meet the centre point, then turn it over and repeat again in the other direction.

12. Repeat with the 5cm wires to make four slightly larger 'S' shapes.

13. Make a loop at one end on each of the 10cm sections.

14. To assemble the windchimes, take a small S hook, put one loop through the hole in one of the teaspoons and pinch shut. Attach the loop on one of the 10cm sections to the other side of the S.

15. Thread on a selection of beads and then bend another loop at the other end.

Repeat with all the small S hooks and long pieces of wire until all the spoons are attached.

16. Attach the four large S hooks on to the lower four holes on the napkin ring (these hooks might need to be slightly smaller or larger

depending on how far the hole is from the edge of the ring). Hang the beaded spoon sections on to each bottom loop.

17. Cut four 10cm lengths of wire and bend a closed loop into one end of each of the pieces. Thread these loops on to the key ring.

18. Slide a bead on the first wire, bend a loop in the end and hook it on to one of the upper holes on the napkin ring. Pinch it tightly shut then repeat with the other three wires before hanging your lovely chimes in a gentle breeze.

FORCING BULBS

I absolutely adore the onset of winter; the shorter the hours of daylight, the more my heart sings, to the disbelief of practically everyone I know. However, sometimes in the depths of foul weather the looming clouds and gloomy light can make even the most ardent winter-lover yearn for just a touch of colour. Beautiful forced bulbs are the answer, as just a few minutes' work in autumn can provide the most glorious flowers to fragrance the darkest days, bringing their sunny little faces into your home just when you need them most.

Forcing is the process which encourages bulbs to flower months early, tricking them into thinking winter has already passed by chilling and leaving them in darkness. The simplest way to plant them at home is to purchase either what are known as prepared

bulbs, such as hyacinths, or those sold specifically for indoor planting. Prepared hyacinths have already been pre-treated with the cold temperatures necessary to kick start them by the supplier (although you can do this yourself by putting them in the refrigerator for five to six weeks. Pop them in a paper bag and store them in the vegetable crisper, but make sure to keep them away from any fruit, particularly apples. These release ethylene gas which can inhibit the development of flowers later on.)

The bulbs are planted in compost and then kept in a cold, dark place for a number of weeks. Once they start to shoot, they can then be brought out into warmth and light, where they will continue to grow and then flower. The time this process takes varies depending on the type of bloom, so if you want them for Christmas, work out how long it takes to force them then work backwards from that in

terms of planting; the last week of September is traditionally the week to plant hyacinths for the festive season. However, as we are dealing with the forces of Nature, nothing is ever an exact science so it is a good idea to plant two or three batches staggered a week apart if you want them for the big day.

Choose bulbs that are firm, and store in a cool, dark place in a paper bag until you are ready to pot them up. Specialist bulb fibre is available, designed for pots without holes, but I think general multipurpose compost works just as well; just add a little gravel or some tiny pebbles at the bottom of your chosen planter to ensure the bulb isn't sitting in a puddle of water.

Although they cannot be forced again, daffodils, hyacinths and crocuses can all be planted in the garden once they have flowered. When their moment of glory has passed, remove the spent blooms and continue to water the leaves. Add a little bulb fertiliser and treat the pot like a houseplant until everything starts to turn brown. At this point allow the pot to dry out completely before removing the bulbs, brushing them clean and storing them in a paper bag in a cool, dark place. Plant again outside after the risk of hard frost has passed (they might not flower brilliantly the first year as they have worked so hard already, but be patient and eventually you should be rewarded).

HYACINTHS (HYACINTHUS ORIENTALIS, JAN BOS AND BLUE PEARL VARIETIES)

- Chill time 10–12 weeks
- Time to flower 2–3 weeks

Method

1. Make sure to purchase prepared bulbs. One point of note with hyacinths is that the bulbs contain oxalic acid which can be irritating to skin and cause a dreadful itch, so do wear gloves while you are working. Choose a pot that is at least 10cm deep and 12cm wide,

and place a layer of grit or small pebbles in the bottom. (If the planter is too shallow the strong roots can push the bulb up and out.) Deep tea cups and mugs work well for single blooms, whereas wide dishes suit multiple bulbs. Only plant single colours in each container as different varieties may take different lengths of time to shoot and flower.

2. Plant the bulbs in moist compost (mixing in a little more grit to help with drainage) so the pointy tops are level with the rim of the container. Leave about a centimetre of the tip protruding from the growing medium. Multiple bulbs should be planted close together but not touching. If you are hoping to give them as Christmas gifts, then the last week of September is the perfect time to start them off.

3. Place in a cold, dark place such as a shed or garage, covered with an old blanket or some newspaper. Less than 10°C is ideal.

4. Periodically check the pot and add a little water to dampen the compost if it has dried out.

5. After about ten weeks, white shoots should appear. Once they reach about 4cm high, bring the planter inside and place in a well-lit but cool location. Dress the pot with a little moss if you fancy.

6. The shoots will turn green, and two to three weeks later your bulbs should flower. Turn the pot occasionally so the blooms don't follow the sun and lean over; if left close to a heat source they can grow too quickly and flop over so keep them away from radiators or other heat sources.

CROCUS (CROCUS SATIVUS)

- Chill time 10–12 weeks
- Time to flower 4 weeks

Method

1. Crocus bulbs are actually called corms; be sure to buy firm ones without a hint of squishiness.

2. Choose a wide, shallow pot with drainage holes (if your beautiful antique chamber pot doesn't have holes, you can plant everything in one that does, and then pop that inside when you are ready to display them).

3. Fill the pot with moist compost and plant the corms so their pointy snouts are level with the rim of the container. Pack them in closely but ensure they are not touching. Move the container to an unheated garage or shed; keep them cool and in the dark, but make sure they don't freeze.

4. Check the corms periodically to make sure the compost hasn't dried out; if it has, moisten sparingly. If the bulbs end up with permanently soggy bottoms they will rot rather unhappily.

5. After 10–12 weeks, when the roots are well developed and shoots have reached a height of about 5cm, bring them into your home and place them in a cool corner out of direct sunlight.

6. After about four weeks, the first flowers should appear; move to a brighter area of your home and turn the container periodically so they don't lean over trying to follow the sun.

PAPERWHITE NARCISSI (NARCISSUS PAPYRACEUS)

- Time to flower 6–8 weeks from planting

Method

1. Unlike hyacinths and crocuses, paperwhites don't need a period of darkness for them to produce shoots. However, as with hyacinths, they can cause an extreme itch to skin so wear gloves as you plant them up.

2. Paperwhites have long root systems so choose tall pots of at least 12cm. Add a layer of small pebbles or grit to the bottom, then add moist compost. Pop the bulbs in so their tips are level with the rim of the container, and their shoulders are just poking out of the compost. They can be packed closely together but don't let them touch.

3. Keep the pot in a cool shed for the first two weeks before bringing it out somewhere warmer, periodically dampening the growing medium if it has dried out. Paperwhites are notoriously tall and leggy, but research by Cornell University has shown that adding a 4–6 per cent solution of alcohol to the watering solution can shorten the stems, preventing them flopping over once they are bearing heavy flowers; simply add one shot of vodka or gin to 7

shots of water, once the shoots are about 2 or 3cm tall. You can also poke some pretty twigs into the pot, to help support the blooms.

4. Once inside, the pot should be kept in a well-lit but cool location, to prolong the flowers.

5. Sadly, paperwhites are not hardy and do not transfer well outdoors, so compost the bulbs once they have flowered.

CAMPFIRE POPCORN POPPER

Arguably the easiest of campfire recipes, and perfect for Halloween or Bonfire Night parties, popcorn cooked over an open fire is guaranteed to keep children happy! An easy popper can be made from two sieves and a little bit of ingenuity; the great thing about making it this way is that not only can everyone gasp in anticipation as the kernels pop, but the corn is also less likely to burn as it's much easier to agitate than when in a pan.

Materials

- 2 metal sieves with those little 'ears'
- Garden wire
- A long stick (I used an old broomstick)
- A 25–35mm metal hose clip (purchased from the village hardware shop)

Method

1. Remove any plastic attachments from the sieves.

2. Attach the bottom sieve to the stick. To ensure your popper doesn't fall off the handle, you can drill two holes in one end of the stick and pass the wire through the holes to attach the bottom sieve securely. Alternatively, if you are using a freshly cut green stick, cut a couple of notches in the wood to achieve the same effect.

3. Put the second sieve on top of the first and wire them together through the two pairs of ears to make hinges.

4. Slide the hose clip up over the stick and both sieve handles. Tighten it just enough so you can slide it up and down to keep the sieves in place while you are popping; at this stage it is useful to attach it with a piece of wire to the handle as well, just so it doesn't fly off into the undergrowth when you least expect it.

5. Add a handful of popcorn kernels into your newly crafted campfire triumph, and close the popper by sliding the hose clip round the handle.

6. Hold the popper above the embers of your fire, agitating it every few moments while avoiding any flames; it needs to heat up quickly to about 180°C, otherwise you will end up with scorched kernels that refuse to pop. (This is because as the kernel heats up, the moisture within turns to steam and this pressure forces the hard skin to split. The kernel essentially turns inside out and the corn starch expands and solidifies, forming the lovely puffy popcorn flesh. Heat it too slowly and the hull will just rupture quietly, without the necessary explosion of steam.)

7. Once the popping has slowed right down, allow your contraption to cool for a few minutes before undoing the catch and tipping the

contents into a bowl. Popcorn cooked in this way will have a lovely smoky, outdoorsy flavour so only needs dusting with a scattering of sugar and a pinch of salt if you fancy.

PRESERVING AUTUMN LEAVES FOR CRAFTS

One of the great pleasures of autumn is kicking and shuffling one's way through crisp piles of golden and russet-hued leaves, even more so when they have been carefully tidied into a pile by a family member.

When left to their own devices, fallen leaves may turn that particular damp shade of brown reminiscent of 1980s school sandals, and therefore are not eminently desirable for crafts. However, they can easily be preserved by soaking them in a solution of vegetable glycerine and water. Over a period of days, the glycerine replaces the water content in the leaves, ensuring they retain their colour well into winter and beyond; they will also remain pliable, and are thus perfect for wreath, mobile and garland making. Glue on to jam jars for a quick candle holder for your Bonfire Night party, suspend from embroidery hoops as a seasonal mobile or use them as gift tags or place holders at a special lunch (they can be written on with paint pens or metallic markers).

When selecting your leaves, pick them fresh from the tree if you can, leaving on a length of stalk if possible (this not only helps to suck up the mixture but can be handy if you need to wire them on to your project). Red leaves may lose some of their colour when preserved and become a pretty shade of pink while green ones will become brown; I have found the most successful to be the leaves of the field maple. Growing wild in woods and hedgerows, it tends to blend into other greenery all summer long, but in autumn its rich shades of gold provide a welcome burst of colour. In folklore, a branch of field maple hung above your door is also supposed to stop bats entering your home.

Materials
- Vegetable glycerine
- Water
- Selection of autumn leaves
- Kitchen roll

Method
1. Select your leaves on a dry morning and brush off any little creatures.

2. Place the leaves in a large bowl or dish, then have a root around in the cupboard and find a plate or similar that will fit inside and keep the leaves submerged in the glycerine and water solution.

3. To create the preserving mixture, stir together 1 part glycerine to 2 parts water; you will need enough to cover the leaves comfortably once they are weighed down. Here I used 300ml of glycerine and 600ml of water, which gave me plenty to cover everything.

4. Pour the liquid over the leaves, give everything a good poke and then place your weight on top.

5. Soak the foliage for between two and five days, checking them every now and then; they should feel soft and pliable when ready.

6. When you are happy with the colour and texture, remove them from the mix and dry carefully on a paper towel. The glycerine solution can be used again, even if it does look a little murky. (Although I have never had a problem, in very high humidity apparently the preserved leaves can weep glycerine a little, so avoid putting them on polished or wooden surfaces.)

RUSTIC AUTUMN MOBILE

This seasonal mobile is formed by twisting a few bendy twigs into a ring, before binding on a selection of interesting dried flowers and twiggy bits salvaged from the garden. Here I have used feverfew (which grows like a weed by my back door) and common sorrel; one of those plants you will probably never notice in summer, as autumn comes around it turns a beautiful shade of dark red, and can easily be found poking its head up in verges and grassland. A lack of enthusiasm on my part for cutting back dead herbaceous plants in flower beds often provides all sorts of unusual shapes and unexpected textures for wreath making.

Preserved leaves are then hung on thin thread; so delicate are

they that the merest breath of moving air is enough to set them fluttering and spinning gently. If you can't face going out in the rain to collect twigs, an embroidery hoop or repurposed grapevine wreath would make a splendid alternative.

Materials

- A few bendy twigs (willow and dogwood are ideal)
- A generous armful of dried flowers, common sorrel and seed heads

- A selection of preserved leaves
- Secateurs
- Floristry reel wire
- Hairspray
- Jute string
- Thin fishing line or cotton thread
- Needle
- 25mm split key ring

Method

1. Take your first twig and bend it into a circle. Holding it firmly at the point where the twigs cross, wind both ends around the circle to make a basic wreath shape.

2. Holding the ring in your left hand, poke your next stick into the ring, from front to back. Once again pinch the twig where it crosses the wreath then wind the rest of the long end round.

3. Continue to add more sticks in this way, gradually working your way around until you are back at the beginning and your wreath has a lovely full structure. Gently push it this way and that until you are happy with the shape, then snip off any unwanted stems to neaten it up.

4. Tie one end of the reel wire on to the wreath, lay on a handful of sorrel and dried flowers then wrap the wire around both the twigs and the stems (just under the seed heads) to bind them together.

5. Lay another bunch of dried material on the wreath slightly further down so it covers the wire, then bind again. Keep adding more bunches and wrapping tightly until you are back at the beginning, then wire the last stems under the first seed heads so they are hidden.

6. At this stage you could of course just leave the wreath as, you know, a wreath, but if you wish to turn it into a mobile it needs to be suspended horizontally. Cut two 75cm lengths of jute twine and tie the end of each one on to the wreath; you might find it easiest to attach it to the binding wire rather than wiggle it all the way through the dried plants.

7. Pass both strings through the split key ring and then tie each one to its opposing side (the fact that the jute cords can slip back and

forth through the ring will help it to be suspended level).

8. Select your favourite leaves and arrange them so the larger ones are ready to hang at the bottom of your first thread, progressing to smaller ones further up.

9. Thread a long length of cotton or fishing line on a needle, fold it in half and knot the end. Starting with the larger leaves, sew four or five on to the thread with one or two stitches to hold them in place; as the leaves have been soaked in glycerine you should find they are lovely and pliable, and won't tear when pierced with a needle.

10. With the needle still attached, stitch the thread on to the binding wire on the inside of the wreath so the leaves can hang freely. Repeat with four more lengths then hang your mobile in the window and watch the leaves gently turn.

SLOW COOKER ROSEHIP FACIAL OIL

Rosehip syrup has long been used to stave off winter colds, thanks to its high vitamin content, but did you know rosehips are a lifesaver for winter skin? Packed full of nutritious vitamins, A, C and E, these and their essential fatty acids work to reduce inflammation and bruises, treat acne, soothe stretch marks and scars and even (and I like this best) reduce the appearance of fine lines and wrinkles.

Pick the rosehips on a sunny morning when they are dry; as with sloes it is always helpful to gather them after the first frost as it makes their skin softer and the flesh sweeter. As the fresh hips contain little hairs which can be irritating to the skin, they need a little preparation before you make your serum; while any rosehips can be used, try and find some of the chunkier ones if you can, as it will save you lots of time when it comes to cleaning them.

Although the hips need to be thoroughly dried before you use them (they have a high moisture content and any water going into your precious oil will cause it to spoil quickly), the dried fruit also makes a beautiful tea. Steep one tablespoon of roughly chopped rosehips in boiling water for 3–4 minutes before straining and adding in a little honey; perfect if you feel as though you are coming down with a winter bug!

As with all foraging, make sure they have not been sprayed with any chemicals and are away from traffic pollution; only take as many as you need. Avoid any rosehips that have started to blacken or that are squishy, and wear gloves to avoid being scratched.

Ingredients

- 1 cup of dried rosehips
- 2 cups sweet almond oil (450ml)
- Amber dropper bottles

Method

1. Prepare your rosehips. Cut them in half and carefully scoop out the seeds and hairs before rinsing thoroughly (if you have very sensitive skin you might like to wear gloves for this).

2. Dry the hips. If you have a dehydrator then dry them according to the manufacturer's instructions, but you can also lay them on a baking sheet and pop them in the oven for 3–4 hours at 50°C until thoroughly desiccated and crispy. I have had great success by putting them on a wire rack above my woodburner, but you could tuck them away in the airing cupboard for a few days too.

3. The facial oil recipe couldn't be simpler. Place the dried hips in your slow cooker, add the almond oil and heat for 8 hours on the 'low' setting (you don't want the oil to heat up too much or all those magic healing properties may be affected).

4. Allow the mixture to cool and stir before straining through a layer of muslin (just in case any hairs have slipped the net!). The easiest

way to do this is by laying the muslin over a jug and securing it in place with an elastic band, then just topping it up as the oil drips through.

5. Store in an amber bottle with dropper to preserve the oils as long as possible, and keep in a cool, dark place.

6. Massage 2–3 drops of oil on to damp skin morning and evening. It works wonders on dry hair if you rub a couple of drops through the ends, and can also be rubbed on to nails and cuticles.

7. The mixture should last up to six months, but if at any point the fragrance changes then discard it as the oil may have gone rancid. I would also recommend you do a patch test first, just in case your skin is sensitive to the ingredients.

Winter

GINGERBREAD SYRUP

Gingerbread is one of the iconic flavours of winter, and this sumptuous syrup is perfect for bringing a touch of spice to your morning coffee. Add to lattes, cocoa or hot apple juice for a wonderfully warming drink, or brush over cakes for a sticky glaze. It makes a delicious addition to breakfast too, poured over Greek yoghurt, porridge or pancakes, and adds a festive twist to cocktails. (A quick note; in a pinch ground ginger makes a perfectly acceptable alternative if you can't be bothered to head out in the cold to get the fresh stuff.)

Ingredients

- 400g brown sugar
- 450ml water
- 2 tablespoons black treacle/molasses
- Strip of orange peel (about 15cm long)
- 6 cloves
- 4 peppercorns
- 6cm chopped fresh ginger root, skin on (or 3 teaspoons ground ginger)
- Cinnamon stick (or 1 teaspoon ground cinnamon)

Method

1. Place the water, sugar and treacle into a large pan and bring to the boil until the sugar has dissolved.

2. Reduce the heat so the mixture is simmering. Bash the cinnamon stick up with a mortar and pestle or the end of a rolling pin, then add this, the orange peel and other spices to the pan. Continue to cook for 25–30 minutes until the syrup has reduced.

3. Allow to cool then filter through a fine mesh sieve.

4. Pour into sterilised bottles.

5. The syrup will keep for up to a month when stored in the fridge; a tablespoonful should be perfect to add a little spice to your morning coffee or evening rum cocktail! It also freezes very well, and can be poured into ice cube trays for popping into cold drinks.

HOW TO FELT A WOOL JUMPER

Have you ever removed a well-loved wool sweater from the washing machine only to find it is now the perfect size for a small toddler? Well, no longer do you have to consign it to the rubbish bin, as from a crafting point of view there is plenty of life still left in it. Console yourself with the thought that it can now be turned into lots of lovely projects, and if you have woolly jumpers you no longer wear, it is relatively easy to ruin them deliberately.

Technically, 'felting' is the process of consolidating loose fibres, whereas here we are actually 'fulling' ready-made fabric using heat, detergent and agitation; as these processes work on the wool fibres they become more and more matted until at last they become bonded enough that the fabric won't fray when cut with scissors.

However, as felting is the term most commonly used to describe the latter practice we will stick with it.

It is important to note that this won't work on synthetic fibres so check the garment label first to ensure that it is at least 70 per cent wool. Place each jumper you wish to felt in separate pillow cases and tie a large knot in the end of each one (the knots will help bash the sweaters about a bit, and if you have a couple of pairs of jeans and an old pair of trainers that you can throw in as well, so much the better). Put them in the drum of your washing machine, add a half-measure of your usual detergent and set the machine to its hottest and longest setting; when removed you should find they have shrunk in size and the fabric is now nicely compacted. Popping them in the tumble dryer for a while on a hot setting should finish the job off nicely.

Snip a hole near one of the underarm seams (where it is least likely to interfere with any sewing patterns) and rub the cut edge; if it frays you may need to repeat the washing process, but if no threads start to unravel then you are ready to start your next craft project. You can generally tell straight away when it needs another session, as the fabric will still feel stretchy rather than tight and you will still be able to identify individual threads. It can often take two or three washes to achieve good results so saving up all your jumpers and doing them in one go is much more economical.

Felt is such a wonderful resource to work with on cold, dark evenings as it is so warm and tactile. All the following winter projects and gifts use home-felted sweaters, but felted wool is readily available from craft shops and makes a great alternative, as would an old pair of denim jeans.

COSY ROSE WREATH

This attractive wreath has a lovely soft quality, made from plump felt roses. Of course, you could wrap a few tiny fairy lights around the flowers for Christmas, but I think it is so cosy looking it would add a touch of Scandi hygge to your home all year round. You could use a ready-made willow or grapevine wreath as a base, but my cardboard version only takes a few minutes to make, using the contents of the recycling bin and some fabric scraps.

Materials
- Felted wool fabric from two men's sweaters (or the equivalent in 3mm felt wool fabric)
- Fabric scissors

- Craft knife
- Hot glue gun and glue
- Stiff cardboard
- Scraps of coordinating cotton fabric ripped into 4cm strips (leftovers from the rag rug project are perfect)

Method

1. Firstly, make your felted roses (we want lovely fat ones so they fill the wreath with a minimum of effort). Cut both sleeves off the first jumper then open them up by slitting along the underarm seam.

2. Cut each one in half lengthways, and trim off the seams.

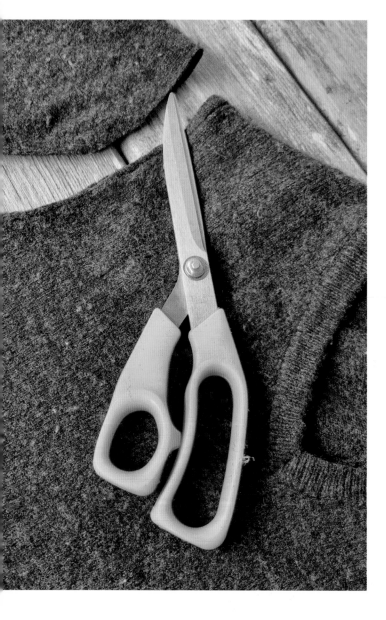

3. Trim off the neck area neatly then cut the front side into four equal strips, removing the side seams.

4. Cut the back section into six equal strips, again removing any seams. Repeat with the second sweater.

5. Trim the collar and set aside, along with one strip from each sweater and any usefully sized scraps.

6. To make a rose, fold a strip in half lengthways, with the ribbed cuff off to the left (if one side of the jumper is very bobbly, make sure the bobbles are on the inside of your folded strip). Fold the right-hand corner down towards you.

7. Starting at this corner, begin to roll fabric towards you, along the folded edge. Add a blob of glue in between the layers to hold everything in place.

8. After a couple of rolls, fold the fabric in your left hand away from you so it folds behind the strip, then continue to roll. Work in this way, rolling and gluing until you have used all the sweater fabric. Don't worry if the base is a gluey mess with excess fabric, this extra material will give your rose some height when you attach it to the wreath.

9. Repeat with the rest of the jumper strips until you have a pile of lovely fat squishy roses.

10. To make the leaves, cut ten basic leaf shapes from your lighter coloured fabric, roughly 9cm long. Repeat with the darker shade, cutting them to about 8cm in length (they don't need to be accurate).

11. Apply a smear of hot glue to one of the darker leaves and then firmly press it on to a lighter one.

12. Squeeze a blob of glue on the base of the leaf then carefully pinch the sides together to give you a furled shape (this also helps make them a little stiffer).

13. The wreath base is cut from a large sheet of cardboard, using a dinner plate (27cm) and a tea plate (18cm) as the template; I would just lay your roses on top of the marked-out base before you cut it, just to check it is approximately the right size.

14. Carefully cut out the wreath using a craft knife.

15. Add a blob of hot glue to the back of the wreath and attach one of the cotton strips. Wind the strip round the cardboard, gluing on new strips as necessary until it is completely wrapped in fabric.

16. Cut a 20cm section from the collar, fold it in half and glue it on to the wreath base to make the hanging loop.

17. Lay the roses on the wreath so you have a rough idea where you want everything to go before attaching them with hot glue. I find it easiest to add the larger

ones first, before snuggling the smaller ones into the gaps. I would also suggest adding adhesive just to the base of each rose when you fix them all in place, before going back over the whole project and squeezing more adhesive into the gaps between each one.

18. Lastly, add a blob of glue to the base of each leaf, before snuggling them down in between the roses to finish everything off.

SNAP COIN PURSE

Handy little snap purses can easily be sewn in batches, and thus make perfect stocking fillers or teachers' gifts. In this version, I have made a small one which is ideal for coins, but you could also make slightly larger ones as covers for E-readers etc. The joy of using felt is that the fabric is so thick it doesn't need lining; thick denim also works very well as it is so sturdy, so an old pair of jeans will provide ample material for this project. (If, however, you are using scraps of thinner fabric, such as cotton, it will probably need a layer of interfacing between any lining and the outer material to stiffen it.)

Two sections cut from an old metal tape measure provide the 'snap' to open the pouch, so if you decide to sacrifice one for the project you will be able to make multiple purses; however, if you don't have anything suitable, flex frames designed for the purpose are available online or in craft shops. As you can see from the photograph, embroidery is not my strong point, but with some old shirt buttons from my granny's button box and some left-over embroidery floss with which my mother made something or other in the 1970s, it was very simple to make a quick design using just chain stitch and running stitch. My grandmother also said that needlework should look as neat from the back as it does on the front, but frankly I am too embarrassed to show you.

Materials

- Fabric scissors
- Old metal tape measure
- Duct or masking tape
- Felted wool jumper fabric (or thick wool felt)
- Buttons, embroidery thread and ribbon to embellish the purse
- Sewing machine or needle and thread

Method

1. Unscrew the tape measure to gain access to the metal strip (it's usually just two or three small Phillips screws). Cut two 10cm sections (use your oldest scissors for this) but please be careful as the edges may well be sharp.

2. Round off all four corners so they won't poke through the fabric then cover with a little duct tape for extra protection. Again, please take care as the little pieces which are trimmed off can be vicious.

3. Cut a section of fabric measuring 12cm wide, and between 30 and 33cm long. The actual length you require will vary depending on how wide your tape measure sections are. Mine were 2.4cm wide so in order to cover them and still have enough room to store my treasures, I cut a 33cm length. Embellish the front with buttons to your satisfaction; just remember that any pretty additions will need to be at least 1cm away from the long edges to accommodate the side

seams, and you are going to lose roughly two and half times the width of the tape measure at the top.

3. Snip two 5cm sections of ribbon so they can be folded in half to make pull tags.

4. Lay the fabric out with the right side facing you. Fold the top shorter edge over towards you by 0.5cm and then fold again, so you have a channel wide enough to fit your metal tape measure through snugly. Tuck one of the ribbons under the seam and then pin everything in place. Repeat with the bottom edge.

5. Sew along both seams as close to the folded edge as you can and then remove the pins.

6. Fold the fabric so the right sides are together then sew up one side leaving a 1cm seam allowance (zigzag up the hem to secure it if you think it necessary).

7. Feed the metal tape measure sections into both channels and then sew up the second seam, ensuring that the numbers are facing away from each other (they need to face each other when the purse is turned inside out in order for it to snap open and shut). Be very careful that the sewing machine needle doesn't crash into the metal tape measure!

8. Finally, turn the purse inside out, poking out the bottom corners with a pencil to finish it off; give a gentle tug on both ribbon tags to open the pouch.

ROSE BROOCH

These soft felt roses are very quick to make and can be used to embellish everything from bags and cushions to bobble hats. As with the snap purse, they are also very effective when made from

old denim, as not only is the fabric good and sturdy, if it does start to fray it just adds to the look! They are made in a slightly different way to the roses in the wreath project, for a slightly less chunky look.

Materials

- Fabric scissors
- Hot glue gun
- Two colours of felted wool
- 3cm brooch back
- French/tailor's chalk if you have it

Method

1. For the rose, draw out a circle on to your felt using French chalk and a small tea plate; it should measure roughly 12 or 13cm in diameter.

2. Start to cut around the circle, but instead of following the line you have drawn, add a scalloped edge as you go. When you are nearly back at the beginning, start to spiral inwards; the distance from the top of the bump to the bottom of the strip should be about 3cm.

As with everything I make, nothing is an exact science until it happens! There is no need to be very accurate, it's just a suggestion of petals we are looking for; the bumpier the scallop, the rounder the petals will be.

3. When you reach the centre of the ring, leave a small tab at the centre. Trim your starting point to a taper.

4. Snip two leaves measuring roughly 6cm x 3cm from your second piece of felt.

5. To assemble the rose, take your first spiral and starting at the tapered end, roll it up until you reach the felt tab. Holding everything tightly together, use sharp scissors and trim the back of the bundle so you have a flat surface (this will stop your rose sticking out too much when you pin it on to your

favourite hat!). You can let everything unroll a little to give you a looser flower if you like.

6. Set your glue gun to the 'high' setting if it has one (but do be careful as the glue will be volcanically hot, and once it sticks to your poor fingers you will struggle to remove it, even as you shriek). Spread a little hot glue over the trimmed edges to hold everything in place (still keeping the tab out of the way) then attach the two leaves.

7. Add a little adhesive to the tab and press over the back to hide all the joins.

8. Glue or stitch a 3cm brooch back on to the rear of the rose before pinning to your favourite coat or cushion.

SWEET ORANGE WINTER BALM

One's lips are always the first thing that seems to suffer as soon as the weather starts to become chilly; the skin here is much thinner and does not produce any oil, so as soon as they are exposed to wind and cold they may become chapped. Keep them soft and supple and protect them from the elements with this fabulous little pot of lip balm, or smooth on to dry and cracked noses for instant relief. Packed with moisturising ingredients it also makes a great gift when packaged up with some rose petal milk bath and a small bottle of rosehip oil.

Small tins specifically designed for lip balms are available to purchase online and in craft shops; however, I love those tiny glass jam and marmalade jars you find at hotel breakfast buffets, so I always hang on to them specifically for this project (they have a capacity of 45–50ml, when you are working out quantities). Here I have used sweet orange essential oil (which is a by-product of orange juice production); make sure you use this rather than orange essential oil as that can make skin photo-sensitive. If you are going to use any other essential oils please make sure they are edible, such as peppermint and spearmint.

Ingredients (enough to fill 3 x 45ml jars)
- 30g (2 tablespoons) soy wax flakes
- 30g (2 tablespoons) coconut oil
- 15g (1 tablespoon) shea butter
- 10 drops sweet orange essential oil

Method

1. Sterilise your containers. Because the jars and lids are so tiny, the easiest way to ensure they are bacteria free is by popping them in a saucepan of water. Bring to the boil so the pan bubbles away nicely for 10 minutes. Carefully drain the water away and set the jars to dry on the counter.

2. Place the soy wax, shea butter and coconut oil in a heatproof bowl and set it over a pan of boiling water. Warm over a medium heat until everything has melted, then stir thoroughly.

3. Allow the mixture to cool for a few minutes before stirring in the essential oil, then pour into your prepared

containers and put on the lids. I find transferring the liquid balm into a tiny jug helps the pouring process to be infinitely less messy.

4. Label and package prettily. The balm will keep very well for at least six months as there is no water content, but do keep it away from sunlit window ledges in the height of summer!

BEADED SNOWFLAKES

I am blessed with a jewellery box full of broken glass bead necklaces that I have managed to accumulate over the years. Some were inherited from my granny and always seemed too special and sparkly to use for everyday crafts, but as they were going to be made into Christmas ornaments I thought it was time to repurpose them. It is always worth a rummage in your local charity shop as they often have long strings of glass beads for just a couple of pounds now they no longer seem particularly fashionable. The snowflakes also look very pretty when made with natural and white painted wooden beads for a rustic Scandi look.

Materials
- Glass or wooden beads
- Silver floristry reel wire (whatever beads and wire you use, the wire will need to pass through inside your chosen bead twice)

Method
1. Cut a length of wire measuring 70cm.

2. Thread six beads on to the wire and slide them up to the centre.

3. Form the beads into a ring, then push one end of the wire through the first bead. Pull it tight to form a circle with two equal tails of wire.

4. Thread four beads on to the right-hand piece of wire, then push the end back down through the first bead; pull tight to form the first point of the

snowflake (you might find it helpful to bend a slight curve into the end so it pokes out between the beads easily).

5. Slide the wire through the next bead on the ring and then out again before pulling tight.

6. Once again thread on four beads. Bend the wire back down and push it back through the first bead on the point before pulling tight and sliding through the next adjacent ring bead.

7. Make one more point with the working tail, then turn the snowflake over and start to use the longer length of wire as your new worker (making the snowflake in two halves, as it were, helps to prevent all sorts of tangling issues!). Continue to bead around the ring until you have six points. Slide the working wire through the last remaining bead on the ring.

8. Pass the other wire through the same bead in the opposite direction. Tuck the wires through a few adjoining beads on the adjacent snowflake points to hide them and then snip off.

9. Cut a 20cm piece of wire and push it through the end bead on one of the points. Lightly twist the two ends of the wire together and fold them flat before snipping off both tails. Slide the knot inside the bead so it is hidden.

10. Once you have mastered the basic snowflake shape, you can begin to make them more complex by adding extra 6mm beads on to the arms or interspersing them with tiny rocaille beads.

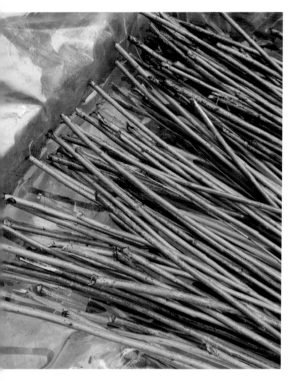

WONDERFUL WILLOW

Willow is a fantastic resource for the crafter, as it ticks all those eco-friendly boxes. Great for biodiversity, fast-growing willow beds are a sanctuary for wildlife and birds, and the nectar and pollen produced provides nutrition for bees and insects. Not only do they stabilise the soil and help slow flooding, they absorb CO_2 during their lifespan; when the withies are cut and crafted, this carbon is trapped rather than being released back into the atmosphere.

Willow has been used for millennia as a basketry material, with archaeological evidence showing weaving techniques dating back 20,000 years. While it can be cut green in winter, the rest of the year I tend to buy buff brown (dried) rods grown on the Somerset Levels. To make the willow supple enough to work with, it has to be soaked in water, the general rule of thumb being that you steep it one day for every foot of its length. Thus a 6ft rod will need to be soaked for six days, then left overnight wrapped in a damp towel or blanket to mellow; it is ready to work with if you can bend a 90-degree angle into the butt end without it cracking or snapping. Keep it wrapped in the blanket while you are working to prevent it drying out too quickly.

Specialist soaking bags are available from suppliers if you don't have a water butt or tank big enough; just don't be tempted to use the bath as it can stain.

WILLOW BUNTING

A lovely addition to your winter garden, this country-style bunting looks so welcoming when twined with a few twinkling solar fairy lights and hung over a porch or front door.

Materials
- 12 soaked willow withies (you could also use other flexible twigs from the garden, such as dogwood, etc)
- Secateurs
- Jute string

Method

1. Snip the first couple of centimetres from the bottom (butt) end of your first withy. Take it in your left hand with the butt facing away from you, then bend the length up and away to the right, at about 20cm.

2. Add another bend at 15cm, and then another, passing it behind the butt end to form your triangle.

3. Now bring this working end round towards the front before wrapping it round and round the triangle, tucking the tip in at the

end; if you can slip it into the point where two other sections of willow cross, you can pull it tight so the end is neatly hidden when trimmed.

4. Fashion eleven more triangles from the remaining withies, then snip off the butts and tips neatly.

5. Cut a length of jute cord roughly 2.5 metres long. Pass one end through one of the top corners of your first triangle and wrap it around the short side two or three times; slide the triangle to the centre of the string, then continue to add the other 'bunts' on either side. Knot the ends of the string into two hanging loops.

WILLOW TREES

Rustic willow trees are quick and simple to make; in this version I drilled holes in a couple of logs to use as a base, but they also look effective in old flower pots; fill with shingle or gravel to weigh the pots down before pushing in the tree. Drape with a little ivy, poke in a few sprigs of holly then wind round some fairy lights for a rustic table centre or mantelpiece ornament.

Materials

- 18–20 soaked willow withies per tree
- A suitable log for a base
- Drill
- 6mm drill bit

Method

1. Take your first willow rod and, with the butt end towards you (resting it on your tummy helps, I find), bend it to the right at about 40cm along.

2. Bend back to the left after another 30cm. Pass it behind what will be the trunk, and then bend again after 20cm; the tip should now point back to the top and you have essentially formed the outline of the tree.

3. Pass the working end down through the first angle you made, round the back of the trunk and out to the left; this should now secure the tree shape, although you will need to keep resting the trunk on your tummy to keep it centred for a couple more rounds.

4. Now begin to weave the working end down and around the left-hand rod, coming back up next to the trunk; go over the top of this and then back down under the right-hand section.

5. Bend the working end back up over the

top of the right rod and then down under the trunk; continue to weave the withy over and under until you have just the tip left.

6. To add a new rod, insert the butt to the left and carry on weaving over and under until you have filled the whole form, pushing the work up as you go so everything is nice and tight. I would just check from time to time that the trunk is still central as sometimes it can drift off in either direction a little, although it is quite easy to nudge it over if necessary.

7. Trim off any unsightly ends using secateurs, angling them so that the cuts are flush with the weaving for a neater finish. Snip a little from the bottom of the trunk too, so it gives a strong blunt end.

8. Drill a hole as far down as you can in the centre of the log and insert the willow tree; you may need to wiggle it around a little to make the hole larger. A blob of PVA or hot glue can be added to the trunk to secure it in the hole if necessary, but I tend to leave them unglued so they can be packed away after Christmas.

WILLOW BIRD FEEDER

This rustic hanging basket can not only be used as a bird feeder but also makes a fun way to store onions, garlic or even satsumas in your rustic winter kitchen. A scrap of drilled wood is used as a jig, or frame on which to work; if you don't have any wood, you can use a piece of stiff cardboard instead. Poke nine holes in a circle, going all the way through the card. Push the withies through the holes so they come out of the other side by 5cm and trim them off evenly; this should give you a stable base on which to work.

Materials

- 4ft to 5ft soaked willow rods (you will need 16–18 for this depending on how dense your weaving is)
- Drill
- 8.5mm drill bit
- Secateurs

Method

1. To make a jig to hold your willow rods, draw a circle 10cm in diameter on your piece of wood and then mark out nine points equally around the circumference (by eye is fine, a few millimetres either way shouldn't make too much difference).

2. Drill nine holes as deeply as you can manage.

3. Snip the bottom couple of centimetres from the butts of nine withies and poke them into holes; as you hold them you will see they have a natural bend, so try and make sure that the curve is facing inwards to give you a pleasing shape.

4. Trim another rod and insert it into the cage you have just made by poking it in behind an upright withy from right to left, over the next one and behind the third.

5. Now start to weave the tip end towards the right, always working over and under until you have reached the end.

6. Insert another rod in exactly the same way as step 4, always poking the new withy in towards the left and weaving towards the right. Once you have woven a band 5cm deep, move 5cm up the rods and start to weave again.

7. Once the second band is finished, snip off all those unsightly butt ends that are poking out; try and cut them at an angle so they are flush with the weave.

8. Cut a 30cm section from the tip end of a new withy in order to tie the bundle together. To do this, hold a 5cm section from the thicker end against the bundle, then use the tip end to wrap neatly around it; push the wispy tip down inside the wrapping and out the other end. Pull both ends tight to secure and then snip off the ends.

9. Carefully remove the project from the jig, and trim the rods neatly at the top.

10. To make the handles, cut two 50cm lengths of willow. Hold them together so you have a thick and a thinner end next to each other. Starting in the middle of the pair of rods and moving outwards, twist the ends in different directions to give a rope effect. Poke the ends down inside the gaps formed by the main frame of the feeder at 12 and 6 o'clock; as the willow dries it will contract and hold the handle in place.

WILD BIRD FAT BALLS

Cheap and nutritious fat balls are quick and easy to make. A wonderful way to encourage birds into your garden during the lean winter months, they also help to eliminate food waste to some extent. Save all your sunflowers once they have bloomed too; hang them upside down to dry for a few weeks and then use the seeds to keep your feathery friends fat and happy.

While the mixture can be used to refill those hanging coconut feeders from the garden centre, it is easily packed into pine cones, old teacups or clean yoghurt pots and hung from a branch (simply make a hole in the base of the yoghurt pot, and thread through a piece of knotted string to act as a hanger before spooning in the mix). The squidgy mix can also easily be rolled into balls, perfect for

your willow feeder. The basic rule for making the mixture is to use a ratio of 2:1 dry ingredients to fat; only lard or suet should be used, as softer fats can affect the waterproofing and insulation properties of birds' feathers.

Ingredients

Lard or suet
Hard cheese, grated
Raisins or other dried fruit
Muesli or raw oats
Seeds or unsalted nuts

Method

As lard comes in 250g blocks, I use an empty 250g butter tub to measure out the dry ingredients so the ratio of 2:1 is vaguely accurate. Simply bring the fat up to room temperature to soften, then squidge through all the other ingredients, either with a spoon or by hand. Roll into balls and chill in the fridge until hard.

ACKNOWLEDGMENTS

Just as it takes a village to raise a child, it also seems to take a village to write a book. Once again, I would like to pass on my heartfelt thanks to all my friends and family who have tasted recipes, foraged for sloes and carted sticks and pine cones through damp woodland. Oscar deserves a special mention for eating French jam in vast quantities in order to keep me supplied with empty jars, as does Heidi for having consistent problems with laundry and ruining so many sweaters and Sue and Elsie for tearing huge amounts of fabric into strips. Nikki, Tobes and Immy, I promised I would put you in here!

My beloved son Wolf, and my dear nephews Noah, Vince, Ottie and Isaac have been invaluable throughout and I love you all.

Dear girls, Sarah, Gem, Angela, Lou and Jen, thank you all so much for your love, help, and constantly putting your recycling in the boot of my car so I could 'do something with it'.

Mummy, Tim, Katy and Dan, I am so grateful for your patience and support while I have been gluing, sawing, muttering, and rooting around in hedges. Last but not least, thanks are due to Cat, who once again has involved herself with great enthusiasm in every project.

ABOUT THE AUTHOR

Becci spent her childhood holidays on the family farm in Denmark, and grew up with a love for all things Scandinavian. Originally, she trained as an archaeologist (Vikings, of course!), before travelling the world and becoming a successful glass artist. She now runs **www.hyggestyle.co.uk,** an online boutique specialising in Danish and Scandinavian gifts, homewares, recipe and craft ideas. She also teaches bush craft, foraging and survival to local schools and youth groups. She lives with her son, cat and chickens, and loves schnapps and herring.